INTER IOR

DESIGN

a professional guide

RIBA ✶ Publishing

Jenny Grove

© RIBA Enterprises Ltd. 2017

Published by RIBA Publishing, part of RIBA Enterprises Ltd, The Old Post Office, St Nicholas Street, Newcastle upon Tyne, NE1 1RH

ISBN 978-1-85946-585-1 / 978-1-85946-827-2 (PDF)

The right of Jenny Grove to be identified as the Author of this Work has been asserted in accordance with the Copyright, Designs and Patents Act 1988 sections 77 and 78.

All rights reserved. No part of this publication may be reproduced, stored in a retrieval system, or transmitted, in any form or by any means, electronic, mechanical, photocopying, recording or otherwise, without prior permission of the copyright owner.

British Library Cataloguing-in-Publication Data
A catalogue record for this book is available from the British Library.

Commissioning Editor: Elizabeth Webster
Production: Richard Blackburn
Design: Bruce Grove
Typesetting: Academic + Technical, Bristol, UK
Printed and bound by Page Bros, Norwich, UK
Cover image: Barnyard, London. Design Brinkworth. Photography Louise Melchior

While every effort has been made to check the accuracy and quality of the information given in this publication, neither the Author nor the Publisher accept any responsibility for the subsequent use of this information, for any errors or omissions that it may contain, or for any misunderstandings arising from it.

www.ribaenterprises.com

About the author

Jenny Grove has worked consistently within the broad field of interiors and architecture, building a long and successful design business and academic career. Working as an interiors consultant for over 30 years since starting out in the 1980s at Wolff Olins, Jenny was also a founding member of one the UK's best known architectural model-making studios and her architectural illustrations have been exhibited at the Royal Academy of Arts and the RIBA. Having previously been course director and lecturer at Chelsea School of Art, Jenny continues to lecture at The Interior Design School.

Acknowledgements

Many people have contributed to this book, and without their time and knowledge it would not have been possible. The project designers and their clients have been exceptional in the help they have given, as have the photographers who have kindly allowed use of their images – thank you to everyone who has tirelessly worked sourcing photographs and permissions and for happily responding to my endless emails and calls. A huge thanks also goes to the peer reviewers for their feedback, and the other designers, architects, writers, colleagues, friends and family who have advised, guided and supported throughout – and to Bruce Grove for the cover design and graphic concept for the book.

Despite my wavering confidence in my skills as a writer, the team at RIBA Publishing has never faltered in their conviction that this book is relevant and needed. My thanks go particularly to Elizabeth Webster, Senior Commissioning Editor, for her gentle yet persistent prompting for its completion and to Richard Blackburn for his tireless attention to production details.

Introduction

When I started out as a designer, the only book available at that time to advise on professional practice was Dorothy Goslett's *The Professional Practice of Design*, which covered professional issues in a very broad and simple way for the design industry as a whole. It did not really help with the specific and often complex issues that arise on interior design projects or running an interior design business, which was never even discussed at college.

I needed help putting interiors in context, to guide me through the intricacies of our profession. Like probably most designers, I learnt on the job, taking models from architecture and other design specialisms.

Since then not a great deal has been written, with the exception of the massive tome edited by Cindy Coleman, *Interior Design: Handbook of Professional Practice*, and several other books by American authors, which are helpful but very US-centric and relevant to their specific regulatory regimes.

In the intervening years no one has written the book that I was looking for, so eventually I took up the challenge myself. The final product is quite different from my original outline, which was more prescriptive. It is not an academic theoretical study, nor does it take a step-by-step approach to tackling a project. The book that has emerged is one that considers interior design in its broadest sense and how it is now a multi-layered, cross-disciplinary global profession which includes design and architecture, cultural, social and business contexts, and how these all impact on decisions and choices.

This book is intended as a useful guide to be referred to regularly, which will help students, practising designers and clients navigate and manage the complexities of undertaking an interior design project.

Chapter 1 examines how history has shaped the profession, how broad in scope interior design is, how it crosses and blurs boundaries, and the importance of intercultural collaborations, authenticity and longevity.

Chapter 2 focuses on the designers' toolkit of creative skills, technical knowledge, communications and collaboration, and business/strategy, and how these all interact and balance to produce successful projects and businesses.

Chapter 3 is concerned with how interior design can and should benefit people, the planet and generate profit: the real core issues of making design a positive contributor to people's lives, improving environments and adding material value.

Chapter 4 concentrates on the relationship between the client and designer in detail – a thorough breakdown of roles and responsibilities, the scope of a designer's involvement, fees and budgets and client contracts.

Having practised and taught in the UK, this book will necessarily have a bias towards British methods, processes and regulations. However, my intention is that I am offering best practice methods, which should be relevant globally to most countries and cultures, by raising issues that need consideration – whether there are regulations or not. Obviously, there will be differing regulations depending on geographic conditions or cultural differences – for example, earthquake building regulations in Japan or Italy, or attitudes towards disability and inclusive design – so the reader needs to understand the principles and make them relevant to where they practise.

A book on this subject matter is by necessity a solid read, so I have included example projects to create visual deep breaths in the text. This goes part of the way to illustrate the broad context in which our profession operates, but these examples are not intended as a demonstration of the best, most high-profile projects that make interiors seem very glamorous. There are a couple like this, but there are also ones that hopefully will engage the reader in considering the impact that interior design can make in the design of hospitals, or residential care for the ageing community, exhibition design and co-design.

My thanks go to all the designers who have kindly contributed and also to those I interviewed and to whom I sent questionnaires – these contributions have added perspicacity and relevance to the text.

Who should read this book?

The main audiences for this book are students and both novice and more experienced designers, all of whom are looking at ways of raising their level of professionalism and the value that they can offer their clients.

It will also be a useful read for:

- clients who are considering engaging a designer and want to understand just what they are undertaking, and
- the *Grand Designs*-esque amateur/property developer to raise issues and processes that they might not be aware of.

To students studying interior design in its broadest sense (interior design, interior architecture, interior decoration, degree and short courses), and novice designers just starting out in the profession (either working within a practice or taking on their first freelance projects), it will explain in detail the project and business management processes and skills that they need to produce successful projects and to run a successful business. It is a complement to the creative skills and processes that they learn at college and will provide a resource to understand that there is so much more to practising successfully as a professional interior designer. While professional practice is a core part of most design courses, it is usually the area of study least enjoyed by students, and largely forgotten until they get into the workplace and realise how much of it is vital to support and integrate into the creative processes that they enjoyed so much at college.

For established designers who have been in practice for many years and have cemented methods and processes that work for them, it might offer alternative ways of thinking about entrenched methods. I hope it will also encourage a review of how their work impacts on people, the planet and profit by enhancing the lives of all those involved in the project, trying to reduce the damaging impact on the environment of the construction industry, and exactly what profit means – it is not just about the money. This book will also serve as a good reference for those working within larger design practices who are not necessarily designers, for example account managers, who will gain a better understanding of the processes involved in a design project.

For clients, or those commissioning an interiors project, the book will be a useful reference to give an understanding of how a project evolves, the processes involved and how best to work with their designer. It will help them realise that their role is an important part of the creative process and how developing a thorough brief and having clear written agreements about who is doing what and when will help ease them through an often stressful process.

The amateur designer/decorator will learn a lot from this book, and it is hoped they will be encouraged to realise that to practise at a professional level they should have some formal training in design or extensive experience with another designer before undertaking projects with clients. However, it will prove an excellent resource for those who undertake their own home renovations or property development by explaining:

- which consultants need to be brought on board
- legislation that needs to be considered
- considerations for engaging a contractor, and
- the detailed thinking and decision-making that is required by the 'designer.'

Defining Interiors

1

Overview

Is it really possible to pin down exactly what interior design is? This chapter will consider the blurred boundaries of the profession and why an absolute definition is a near impossibility. The healthy cross-disciplinary activity that is interior design today is so broad in scope and influence that it is now a culture of specialisms and collaborations of inter-related design professions, rather than a singular profession. Likewise, the discussion about what we call our profession seems to continually rage with various sectors trying to differentiate and protect themselves by creating a hierarchy of terms, such as interior architecture and spatial design, to try and intellectually distance themselves from the persistent shadow of the amateur interior designer/decorator.

To a large extent, the majority of the practising profession do not really worry about what they call themselves because their work encompasses so many design disciplines – the design of interiors and products, furniture, graphics and even architecture – which makes the boundaries of interior design very blurred. In my opinion, it is this fluidity of boundaries which makes the profession as vibrant as it is today, and we should encompass and embrace the fuzziness that allows interior design to push and question these boundaries instead of trying to regulate and control it.

The chapter is divided into four sections:

1. History shapes the profession
2. What is interior design?
3. Cross-disciplinary and intercultural collaborations
4. Authentic long-term versus fashion-led short-term

The aim is to look at interior design, and design in general, from a wider perspective and discuss the ever-changing intercultural and societal challenges that continually reshape the profession.

History shapes the profession

Before the twentieth century the 'profession' of interior design did not exist. It evolved via decoration and through social and political changes, availability of education and the revolutions in mass production and communications.[1] To place interior design as it is practised today into its historical context, here is my unqualified quick romp through the history of interior design.

Interior design's origins were in scene painting, furniture and upholstery. Then, during the eighteenth century the architect took control and designed both interior and exterior, for example the work of Robert Adam. With the arrival of the Industrial Revolution, mass production gave the new aspiring middle classes, who were anxious to communicate their new found prosperity, access to affordable furniture and furnishings. Around the turn of the nineteenth and twentieth centuries came the female amateur untrained society decorator and homemaker (Elsie de Wolfe in the USA being one of the pioneers[2]), and the rise of the Modernist Movement where there was 'no room for cushions'.[3] This, perhaps, was the start of the persistent perception of male, trained professional (usually architect) and female, amateur residential decorator.

This oversimplification of the history and gender stereotyping of early interior design, followed by two world wars, bring us to the mid-twentieth century and it was in the 1950s and 60s that the profession of contemporary interior design became established and taken seriously. This was an era of massive growth in personal wealth, disposable income, the power of the advertising agency, the birth of feminism and equal opportunities for women, and developments in materials technology that enabled the design and manufacture of exciting furniture and experimental buildings.

The late 1960s was the time of Stanley Kubrick's *2001: A Space Odyssey*, when the prototype of Concorde was unveiled and when the Apollo space mission put a man on the moon. After post-war austerity and with these social and cultural developments that looked to the future and the new, there was an air of optimism and a shift towards the modern and experimental. The use of materials developed in the early part of the century and during the wars started to be used in mass-produced furniture design, for example laminated plywood,[4] plastics[5] and fibreglass. Mid-century Modern design was the outpouring of all this optimism and wealth, and made modern design available to those who dared to be different.

The 1960s culture of youth and fashion, sex, drugs and rock'n'roll created new opportunities for the design of retail outlets, restaurants, bars and the such – many being designed by the fashion designers, furniture makers, owners or artists who wanted something other than the traditional and were prepared to take the risk of creating something new. Many of these became successful businesses because of the design of their products and shops, and the lifestyles they promoted, such as Terence Conran and Habitat, Barbara Hulanicki and Biba.

It was around this time that business in a broader sense began to realise the potential of design generally and how it could contribute to its business strategy. The early corporate identity studios (for example, Wolff Olins, founded in 1965 by designer Michael Wolff and advertising executive Wally Olins) combined graphics with marketing and strategic business analysis, providing a seamless corporate identity for its commercial business clients. Olins described corporate identity as 'strategy made visible by design'.[6] Wolff Olins's pioneering clients, such as Apple Records (1968) and Volkswagen (1978), realised that the strategic use of design would differentiate them from their competitors – the design of their products, their brand and their services. It was not until later in the 1970s and early 80s that the interior was recognised as integral to the brand and where the brand became more than a logo. It became a total experience of physical space, product, communications and business strategy to reflect the brand values. This was the turning point for commercial design that saw a massive growth across all design and branding sectors, and when the interior design *profession* started to distance itself from its residential roots.

Design in general benefited hugely from the wealthy 1980s when anything was possible, the budgets for design were huge and everyone wanted 'design'. The aspirational society grew in developed nations: people wanted to live in better homes, travel, drive fast cars, have the first 'brick' mobile phones and wear designer clothes. This superfast charge into making money was very well expressed in the film *Wall Street* (1987), where Gordon Gekko said those iconic words: 'greed is good' and 'money never sleeps'.

Property prices in the UK started to boom. Homeowners began to see the potential for property as a form of investment rather than it being a home for life, which gave rise to the amateur property developer. Global travel became easier and cheaper, with the resultant need for quality hotel accommodation for this new generation of design-aware and wealthy consumers.[7] The political climate was changing in the former Eastern Bloc countries, with the fall of the Berlin Wall in 1989 opening up new markets. The explosive growth of personal computers, electronic and internet technologies led to the new digital design era, with the first personal computer to use a visual interface, the Macintosh 128K, introduced by Apple in 1984.

This all contributed to generating a big market for design and it is perhaps since then that design has in some ways become devalued. Marketeers realised that anything using the word 'design' or 'designer' would be more attractive to this aspirational society – whether or not there was any meaningful design being used. The use of these words appeared to grow in direct correlation to the recognition of the value and the power of the brand, with companies building their brands to attract aspirational buyers who wanted luxury lifestyles or fun or youthfulness. This created brands that had an inflated monetary value over and above that of the product and this has been called 'brand equity mania,'[8] where companies were were often vastly overvalued because they were selling a brand name rather than a product.

Since then there have been several economic booms and busts, with design and branding often being used as a surface filler to gloss over the cracks of an ailing company or product in order to try and make a quick buck in the property markets or to command a premium price for a product that has the name of a 'designer' attached to it.

Our globalised markets demand constant growth – with their inevitable cycles of boom and bust, growth and recession – which will always impact on and influence the design professions. The turbulent years since the 1980s show a recession pretty much every ten years, culminating in the great recession which began in 2008/09, and tested even the strongest design businesses and brands. The International Monetary Fund has said that 'this global crisis caused a dramatic collapse in world growth and the most severe global recession since the 1930s.'[9]

This book cannot hope to inform the reader in any depth about the monetary and political vagaries of our global economy, and how the design professions have been buffeted by these market forces in the last 40 years, making them change and evolve at an almost out-of-control speed. But perhaps since the last great recession, we may have reached a place where design is being revalued. The emphasis now is on creating sustainable services, products, interiors and businesses that are not quite so susceptible to market forces, that do not add to the disposable mentality that damages our planet, that add quality of life to users and inhabitants, and, yes, should still be a significant contributor to the economic prosperity for everyone involved – not just the main stakeholder client as in the past, but all the micro-stakeholders of makers and communities.

What is interior design?

The profession of interior design and the projects concerned with it are ambiguous and shifting. Nothing is fixed or constant, the unexpected is expected. Interior designers have to be flexible and able to change direction as projects unravel and develop. The same applies to their profession – it is a constantly shifting mélange of people and issues that changes with social and economic pressures, contextual challenges and the needs and desires of people.

Many have tried to define interior design, including international and national interior design societies and organisations, but because it is so broad in scope and potential they generally tend to either over-define or over-simplify it – neither being particularly helpful. For example, the simplest Oxford English Dictionary definition is:

The art or process of designing the interior decoration of a room or building.

The National Council for Interior Design Qualification, NCIDQ (examination board for North American interior designers), goes further and describes the problem-solving nature of design. This is expanded upon and explained in great detail on the NCIDQ website:

Interior design is a multifaceted profession in which creative and technical solutions are applied within a structure to achieve a functional, safe and aesthetically attractive interior environment.[10]

One of the best descriptions that touches on the furthest reaches of the powerful influence of interior design is by Graeme Brooker (head of programme, Interior Design, at the Royal College of Art, London):

'Interior Design explores the diversity of human inhabitation in numerous environments, extending from the city to the room ... the interior is an interface between its occupants and the built environment and it supports the notion that the interior is an agent for social change.'[11]

Interior design encompasses everything from a one-room project to the largest corporate office; it can be as complex as architecture or as relatively straightforward as decoration. The scale and complexity of projects might define specialisms within interior design that relate to the designer's level of education and experience (for example, interior architecture, interior decoration, spatial design), but the overarching fact is that interior design covers this gamut of projects which all involve the **design** of the **interior** of **buildings**:

- **Design** is the process of questioning, investigation, curiosity, discovery, analysis, problem-solving and perseverance, applicable across the various design professions.
- **Interior** describes the human environments that we inhabit and their social impact, so the understanding of how people live, work, play, their needs, desires and aspirations.
- **Building** – we nearly always have an existing context to work with, a building to be re-used or an architect's designs for a new build, so we have to understand architecture, its history and social contexts, construction and materials, in order to adapt it and respect it.

Whether we are an interior decorator, stylist, architectural designer, hotel designer, retail designer, exhibition designer or event designer, we work with these three elements. Knowledge of them and how to manoeuvre within them is what makes us interior specialists.

Interior design reaches all parts of our home, working and social lives. It is practised by professionals and amateurs. It is huge in scope and influence. Routes into practising interior design are as varied as the specialisms of interior design, and are often unorthodox – a degree in an interiors subject is not a prerequisite. Many successful practising interior designers today have come from related design professions where a move to designing interiors seemed like a logical next step.

For example:

Adam Brinkworth, founder of Brinkworth, came from a furniture-making and design background, the legacy of which is an acute attention to detail and materials in the firm's work.

Meriel Scott, founder of Precious McBane, has a fine art background and has the most wonderful 'nose' for extraordinary pieces of art and furniture to complement her daring interiors. Likewise, her partner Victoria Wimpenny came from a different direction and studied cabinet-making. This gives Precious McBane's work a bespoke feel for quality, materials and attention to fine details.

Oliver Marlow, founder of Studio TILT, came from a making background (his father was a carpenter). This, combined with an English Literature degree and an MA in Critical Practice in Design, gave him the analytical thinking and making skills which eventually led him to the codesign process he pioneered.

Precious McBane

Apartment, Paris, France

A Parisian weekend getaway in the La Marais district for a London-based client, the tiny apartment on first viewing was clearly much in need of renovation, but also hugely promising – full of light, with high ceilings and beautiful wide oak floorboards throughout. Alongside these raw ingredients, a few of the client's key pieces needed to be accommodated within the scheme: a sofa bed in a slate blue leather, a wooden desk (home from home for a busy working woman) and a large antique rug in soft shades of pink. The design was informed by the client's favourite Dipytque room scent, Baies, smokey and feminine with a modern restraint.

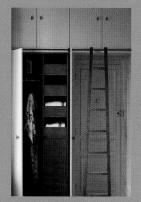

The intention was to create a highly personal space which functioned as the most beautiful backdrop – as well as the most brilliant valet – to the client's every need from the moment she walked through the door with her suitcase (bespoke floor-to-ceiling cabinetry hiding a myriad of space-saving storage details).

The finished space, already blessed with light, was softly illuminated with powder grey walls. The natural light was picked up further by the upholstery in faded golds and bronzes, smokey blues and jewelled amber colours, which enlivens the space. The sofa, with its strong slabs of leather, was made welcoming with a composition of silk and velvet cushions, the trims and textures adding subtle detail and layering. The quiet floral details in the antique rug are echoed in the choice of fabric on the two bolster cushions, one an intense woven silk of peacock feathers, the other gold silken sunflowers embroidered on dark linen (a hand-stitched laundry bag in the same fabric hangs on the bedroom door, one of many detailed touches to harmonise this tiny open-plan space). The dark structural accents in the living area are provided by a Mouille floor lamp and a pair of Adnet leather-framed mirrors, a Cherner armchair in walnut and a bespoke library ladder.

The client refers to the apartment as her 'jewel box'. At night, this jewel box glows as, one by one, the table lamps are illuminated. No computerised circuitry here; the apartment could be nowhere but Paris.

Meriel Scott co-founded Precious McBane in 1993 and works with design partner
Victoria Wimpenny and staff across a variety of residential and commercial projects, as
well as bespoke textiles and furniture.

Precious McBane is recognised for its original British design output. The studio has
maintained a tradition of absorbing talent from outside the world of interiors where the
disciplines of art and sculpture combine to create environments that are reassuringly
warm, detailed and layered with visual interest. Links with other creative disciplines are
further echoed in collaborative works with artists for the studio's private clients, helping
to create unique interiors, particularly as beautiful backdrops to collections of art.

Precious McBane
www.preciousmcbane.com

This cross-disciplinary background of many designers practising today makes interior design a vibrant, rich and unconventional profession. The range of practitioners, including architects, artists, furniture designers, architectural designers, decorators, and exhibition and set designers, means it will never be a contained and easily defined profession. So perhaps it is better just to talk about interior design, or even just 'design', instead of getting fixated on the nomenclature that differentiates one specialism from another. Zeev Aram, of Aram Designs, said during an interview at The British Institute of Interior Design's 2015 conference that

'we should just call ourselves designers and not get hung up on which specialism. We are trained to identify problems and solve them creatively, and this way of thinking can be applied to the largest and smallest of projects across any sector or discipline – if it's not your specialism, work with someone who is a specialist and broaden your collaborations.'

Dutch designer Marcel Wanders has an inspiring attitude to this whole debate. In a *Dezeen* article[12] he says:

Getting caught up in the labels of architect and designer prevents creative people from enjoying someone else's different opinion and trying to study and learn from it'

And continues:

architects have become preoccupied by the exteriors of buildings, and don't give much thought to the interiors. We don't make architecture, we start inside, we start with the human experience.

This broad and generous attitude to designing interiors does not converge with many of the national and international interior design associations that exist around the world. There is certainly a place for professional bodies that represent and support practitioners, however the attitude of some seems to be one of reduction and containment, regulating who can and cannot practise, exactly how much education is required and restricting the use of the title 'interior designer' or 'interior architect.' This level of regulation already happens in many countries in the EU and USA. So far, the UK is not regulated and, in my opinion, is a more experimental and boundary-busting profession because of it.

The International Federation of Interior Architects/Designers (IFI)[13] has a global positioning statement that defines an interior designer as:

'Qualified by education, experience and applied skills, the professional Interior Architect/Designer accepts the following responsibilities: Identify, research and creatively solve problems pertaining to the function and quality of the interior environment; Perform services relating to interior spaces including programming, design analysis, space planning, aesthetics and inspection of work on site, using specialized knowledge of interior construction, building systems and components, building regulations, equipment, materials and furnishings; Prepare schematics, drawings and documents relating to the design of interior space, in order to enhance the quality of life and protect the health, safety, welfare and environment of the public.'

This definition reinforces the idea of the designer as expert in every aspect of a project and doesn't acknowledge the necessary input of other people and professions into the process. The writing implies the role of the designer is to impose their designs onto people to enhance their quality of life rather than embracing the notion of collaboration and societal and cultural understanding. Whereas in reality interior design is an embracing, expansive profession – we collaborate, we learn, we cannot do it alone, we are always part of a team whose combined effort creates the reality. It is a profession that crosses borders – design disciplines, cultural, professional and geographical. The quality of the work and the experience and skill of the people doing the work are the benchmarks for professional standards in the industry, not regulatory bodies who want to try and fit all these odd-shaped designers into a square hole.

Cross-disciplinary and intercultural collaborations

Much interior design results from cross-disciplinary collaborations from within and around the design professions. It is also intercultural, where people from different countries, professional backgrounds, generations, interests and specialisms work together, for example where global markets allow international collaborations on projects, where non-design professions contribute expertise and advice, where generations work together from differing age perspectives, where clients and users collaborate with designers to co-design their spaces. Design is fundamentally all about people – clients, users, consultants, contractors – and therefore it feeds on these collaborations. The differences that are a part of each culture will challenge preconceptions and are what can produce unexpected, appropriate and startling designs.

These social and cultural collaborations will be essential in addressing some of the challenges that are beginning to shape our world. We are entering an era where the ageing population is placing a huge strain on health and care services. The planet is now clearly showing signs of the damage that we have wreaked by industrialisation. Owning a home is getting further out of reach for many, or is an impossibility in many regions of the world. The divide between rich and poor is now so extreme that the minority super-rich is in control of the vast majority of the world's wealth. The size of homes in cities is decreasing due to overpopulation and high property prices. Skill shortages in some professions and trades mean employers are having to think creatively about how to retain staff – especially in the ever-expanding digital world. Business profit margins are being squeezed by lower prices and higher overheads and competition from abroad, so staff are being required to work more efficiently.

These changing demographics of who we are designing for and the resultant social consequences are having a direct impact on what we design and how we design. Examples of this are as follows:

Ageing populations

In 2014, 26% of Japan's population was estimated to be over the age of 65, and it is estimated that by 2060 the over-65s will account for over 40% of the population.[14] The birth rate is continuing to drop, and the burden this ageing population will put on family members as well as the state and how it will affect the economy is of great concern. However, the Japanese tend to stay healthier for longer and work well past 65, but like most developed countries the family unit is no longer localised and finding alternatives to the support that family members used to provide is a big challenge. This is creating a large market of designing for the elderly and creating communities in care homes.

In the Netherlands there is an innovative scheme where students can live for free in care homes on the basis that they spend a certain number of hours voluntarily socialising with the residents, carrying out tasks the staff do not have the time to undertake, such as playing games, having a chat, shopping and just hanging out. This has obvious inter-generational benefits for both the students (no rent) and the residents (social interaction with different generations). The feedback from the majority of the students is that it is not a chore to do their voluntary hours; they really enjoy the relationships that they form with the residents.[15] This inventive solution prevents the elderly from being cut off in care ghettos, but will need inventive design solutions to suit the needs of both generations.

Park Grove Design

The Royal Star & Garter Residential Home, Surbiton, UK

Park Grove Design has been working to raise standards of design in environments for older people for nearly two decades. The principles of 'inclusive design' and the design of welcoming spaces where there is no need for adaptations due to limited mobility, dexterity or sight are central values of the practice founded by Lori Pinkerton-Rolet. With no prescriptive style, they interpret the needs of their clients and the style of the property into effortlessly sophisticated, high-quality interiors.

The Royal Star & Garter Homes is a charity with a mandate to provide outstanding nursing and therapeutic care to the British ex-service community, where the residents are mainly wheelchair dependent or suffer from dementia. Unusually for a care home facility, the majority of residents are men.

The design of the Surbiton Home responds to the historic nature of the Arts and Crafts building, and bases the colour palette on military insignia – colours both uplifting and easy for older people to see. Many different aesthetic environments enable residents to enjoy a variety of activities and experiences. A café and bar encourages residents to play games on the integrated chess and backgammon tables, watch *Match of the Day*, and relax with friends and visitors, with a chalkboard for leaving each other messages – all helping to create a sense of community. A library with computer facilities, newspapers, audio books, a room for lectures and several lounges with differing colour and furnishing schemes provide further social spaces – one with a grand piano. The dining room has a feel of a restaurant, with screens providing intimate spaces for the residents.

Colour is used to help personalise the accommodation. Doors to the residents' rooms are like front doors, with their own colour and brass door-knocker. Fifteen room schemes were developed from which residents could choose their personal room environment. The research for this included prototyping the rooms for the dementia residents for feedback from the residents, staff and relatives to help choose their living environment.

The dementia floor is separated into three 'family' groups relating to severity of the resident's condition. Each family area has a unique and saturated wall colour in accordance with Dementia Care Matters' principles, with themed memory area displays

and open-sided shelving with display items providing interactive stimulation. There are personal memory boards adjacent to each resident room to assist with room location and identity. Items such as a (safe) sewing kit or workbench tools, which relate to the background of each resident, can be found in the lounges. The dementia floor wraps around an enclosed external terrace.

Park Grove Design
www.parkgrove.co.uk

Single living

More people are living alone (or want to live independently), which requires more one-person housing or shared living environments, creating opportunities for the smart design of small space micro-living and communities. Young people wanting to live in cities often cannot afford the high rents, so opportunities for small community living are being explored. For example, New York City ran an architectural competition in 2012 for the design of a new housing model for the small household population. The winning scheme by nArchitects consists of a series of modular apartment units of 23–34 sq m for one or two people, and has community spaces such as a rooftop garden, lounges, a deck, laundry, bike store, café and fitness room.[16] This was among the first of what is now a burgeoning market, which has its drawbacks as many are now being bought/rented as second homes by wealthier people to have a city base, and there are questions about how it is normalising living in spaces smaller than many consider to be healthy.

Pressures on health care systems

It is thought that the economic costs of obesity alone will double nearly every decade. So staying active and healthy, both physically and mentally, can make an impact on individual health and national economies, and good design can encourage this. The Design Council in the UK has a service, 'Active by Design', where it

'work[s] with national and local government, developers, designers and communities to put health and wellbeing at the heart of change in the physical environment. Using evidence and local data, we help our clients tackle preventable diseases and health inequality by building health into existing places and new developments. This means shaping buildings, streets, public spaces and neighbourhoods so that healthy activities are integral to people's everyday lives – not an add-on.'[17]

In New York, the Center for Active Design uses health research and an evidence-based approach to develop activity and healthy communities.

Active Design builds on health research showing that design can impact today's biggest challenges around the physical, mental, and social well-being of communities around the world.[18]

Finding ways of encouraging people to move and be active both mentally and physically should be ingrained in the design of interiors.

The number of people with mental health, psychological and emotional wellbeing issues is increasing. It is a major cause of disruption and difficulty in many people's lives. One in four people will suffer from a mental health issue, which can range from severely disabling conditions to minor emotional stress. For example:

- adolescent issues
- men's mental health
- women's mental health
- Autistic Spectrum Disorder
- learning disabilities
- neuropsychiatry
- dementia.

In the UK, the current economic burden of this aspect of healthcare costs £70–100 billion per year and accounts for 4.5% of GDP. Most people do not require residential care and can recover alone or with the support of their family doctor. Only those with more serious conditions need specialised care or admission. It is time to think differently about how mental health conditions are treated and how interior design can contribute to the recovery of those suffering with them.[19]

Communities and families

The ease of global movement impacts on extended family life. Communities are more transitory, yet people need to feel a part of a group (whether intellectual, physical or emotional) to reduce social instability, social isolation and the accompanying mental health issues. On a very fundamental level, something as seemingly simple as incorporating benches into a design can encourage social interactivity. They can be used as a place to rest, to meet, to chat to a stranger, to pause, to feel a sense of belonging, to be alone, to be together, to watch, to wait – in public spaces, in workplaces, in social spaces.[20] Research shows that the building of housing developments, whether private or publicly funded, do not thrive in early years if there is not an infrastructure already in place of social spaces, transport, shops, schools, community meeting places, gardens and open spaces, along with the less obvious types of support that make people feel at home, such as cultural activities with people who connect other people and encourage them to meet their neighbours, baby-sitting networks, activity spaces, etc. Co-designing in these types of developments is key if they are to become real communities, to allow people to feel ownership and connected.

If these are not provided at an early stage, the communities will not be socially sustainable and will not thrive.[21] Conversely, there is a case for design that does not include any nod to social communities – the fabulously expensive city apartments for the super-rich who like to feel exclusive, disconnected and secluded.

Lifestyles

Re-appreciation of simpler lifestyles and the art of making and growing and having access to nature serves as a relief from the daily grind, eases the environmental impact of mass-produced products and reduces levels of stress. The emergence of craft and one-off makers versus the mass-produced, a place for plants and being in touch with nature are all beneficial. For example, Biophilic Design encourages accessibility to nature, green spaces, light and air. Interface Carpets[22] has a collaborative website and research portal called 'Human Spaces', which discusses many of these issues in its report 'Human Spaces: Global Research into Biophilic Design'.[23] In one section it discusses integrating nature into the workplace:

'We know there is an instinctive bond between human beings and other living systems. Much research into biophilia supports the positive impact that this nature contact can have. Studies have shown the diversity of that impact includes increasing a customer's willingness to spend more in a retail environment, increasing academic performance amongst school children and even reducing anxiety and stress before medical procedures.'

These are just a few of the intercultural and societal issues that design is being challenged to address – especially interior design and architecture. At the core of the challenge is how designers work with these users and communities to understand the issues and design for these challenges. People have always been the focus of interior design, but there is now a more scientific approach being taken to understand the users' needs and desires through the specialisation of social anthropologists working directly with architects and designers. Their quantitative methods for gathering data on how people move, work, live and occupy space is a benefit to many design companies whose clients are addressing some of the cultural issues above.

Gemma John is a social anthropologist who later studied interior design. She has a PhD from the University of St Andrews and was a post-doctoral researcher at the Centre for Research on Socio-Cultural Change (CRESC) at the University of Manchester. Here she explains how she has become a specialist working in interiors and architecture, and how social anthropology contributes to the design of buildings and interiors:

'From my experience, architects and interior designers are interested in understanding the "relationship" between buildings and people, signalling the need for more research in this area, which provides an opening for a social anthropologist to work amongst them.

'As a social anthropologist, I spend time with people to gain insight into the way in which they engage with the built environment. For example, how do people conceive of "collaboration" in a collaborative economy, and how does it affect how we design co-working or co-living spaces?

'Whenever I have the opportunity, I join forces with researchers in academic institutions to gain a deeper understanding of the way in which socio-cultural change affects how we think about and use the built environment. At the moment, I am co-designing a project with the Royal College of Art Helen Hamblyn Centre for Design that focuses on "adaptive" housing for an ageing population. We are particularly interested in understanding what our research participants mean by "adaptive". I am also working with Goldsmiths and Royal Holloway on a bid for an interdisciplinary project on 'pop-up' welfare. We want to understand how people experience temporary architectural structures, and what new understandings of welfare emerge from this in relation to housing, libraries and law.

'I have also recently set up a network that focuses on the intersection between social anthropology and architecture which provides participants with a platform for a cross-disciplinary conversation. Together, we hope to identify shared challenges, and questions, that enable us to build more inclusive cities.'[24]

Likewise, collaborative design, human-centred design and codesign are other emerging specialisms. Designers spend significant time with the users to understand their needs, their existing environments, what they would like to change, to encourage them to contribute and be involved in the design process through workshops and prototyping, and by taking responsibility for their environments. One of the project examples in this book, the NHS Whittington Hospital Trust Ambulatory Care Centre (see pp. 83–86), is an example of the codesign process. Oliver Marlow of Studio TILT explains:

'Codesign transforms the relationship that people have with space and each other through the design process; it engages the end-users in designing and delivering their spaces. It enables communities to deliver a physical space and also understand how that space relates to them. Codesign is a tool that uses design techniques and tactics to solve complex problems. It establishes insight and it synthesises and works with this insight to effectively enable people to come to agreements.'

In his book, *Codesigning Space*, written with Dermot Egan, Oliver describes the start of the codesign process:

'To begin the process, a programme of codesign workshops was established with representatives from all the key stakeholder groups including patients, staff and management. The workshops were facilitated by TILT and utilised its unique codesign activities and tools, helping participants to explore design ideas for the space, including layout, furniture and spatial flow. Through the process, these ideas were transformed into scaled physical prototypes by the workshop participants using basic materials such as cardboard, paper and modelling clay.'[25]

These intercultural issues are just a few examples, but ones that design should and can address to benefit society in a broader context. This all means a refocusing on the user, who is not necessarily the client. It is the users whose lives will benefit if they have a good environment in which to live, work, relax, stay healthy or recover. Gaining an understanding of these issues can only come from collaboration with the users, with those who are going to be inhabiting these spaces. Designers and architects generally believe that they are designing for users, but in reality a great deal of design is to satisfy their own egos, and this is one reason why much design has become devalued. A true appreciation of the input of the users demands open-mindedness on the part of the designer and a real willingness to allow them to contribute – it is this combination that challenges preconceptions and has the potential to produce extraordinary interiors that will be meaningful, have longevity and will not be based on fashion and trends.

Authentic long-term versus fashion-led short-term

In my short romp through history, above, I mention the stereotyping that for many years created a shadow over the profession of interior design – the untrained amateur residential designer. There is still this unwritten attitude today, and perhaps this is a key reason why the national associations would like to regulate the profession of interior design: to remove it from the stigma of amateurism.

To pander to these amateur designers, a whole raft of magazines became popular – from *House & Garden*, one of the earliest publications which was first published in the USA in 1901, to *Elle Décor* (founded 1989) and *World of Interiors* (founded 1981), which created an attitude to design that was based on fashion and trends, and arguably partly culpable for the disposable nature of much residential design. Alongside this is the aspiration of home owners who use property as a form of investment and can buy cheap, do up, sell, make a profit, and move onwards and upwards – with little thought about the buyers coming in and ripping out what was new just a few months ago to satisfy their own aspirations and fashion-likes.

Much residential interior design has an air of disposability about it, exacerbated by some TV shows of the 1990s that made everyone think they could be an interior designer if they owned a staple gun.

We still have today the same thing that was happening around the beginning of the twentieth century, where the wealthy middle classes aspired to live like the wealthy aristocracy. Today we have the super-rich whose lives are splashed across *Hello!* magazine and social media and – like clothes fashion – imitated for a connection to that lifestyle. However, if we can take a back step on trends and dig deeper into the human psyche we will produce interiors that have longevity, will have meaning to the occupants, and will not add to the vast amount of waste that a disposable attitude creates.

Our world is diminishing. We can travel anywhere at anytime both in reality and virtually. We have 24-hour access to all kinds of media and communications. Our appetite for the new, the different and experimental is voracious. The speed of change and knowledge-learning is stratospheric, thanks to the power of the internet, but this constant need for change, to have the newest piece of tech equipment, leads to a disposable attitude both emotional and physical, which is contagious and spreads to other areas of our lives. Change is good, but the fast rate of change is questionable. Think how slow food, slow fashion, having an allotment, growing things and making things are all making a comeback. Are we tiring of the speed with which we must live our lives?

This is a question that is relevant to all areas of our lives – where we live, how we live, where we work and how we work, how we relax, how we recharge, where we go to do this and what activities we do to do this, who we want to spend time with, how we socialise and feel part of a community. These are all essential questions that affect the design of the interiors that we inhabit and are fundamental to creating meaningful and lasting interiors. It is not about wanting offices like Google (we are not Google), or living like a film star, or having a yellow sofa because that is what this year's colour happens to be.

Interior design is not about imposing trends (but it is inevitably influenced by fashion) that are short-term and oftentimes trite. It is about deep investigation into the people who will use the spaces and make them fit for purpose in both the short- and long-term, which makes aesthetics integrated into the process, not leading it. It is about creating meaningful responses to the needs of the users and clients. And it is about recognising the potential of re-using buildings and making them a long-term answer to fulfil and exceed the expectations of the users and clients, and to protect them for the future.

MoreySmith

Red Bull Head Office, London, UK

MoreySmith's design of Red Bull's Head Office has created an innovative and highly inventive workspace that reflects both the character of the brand and that of the old building which successfully marries old with new. The new space reflects the brand's love of sport, music and the arts and provides an energised and creative workspace with excellent facilities and much improved common areas.

Nicola Osborn, design director, MoreySmith

The brief for Red Bull's new headquarters was to create a dynamic, brand-led work environment that would match the vision of Red Bull, reward its staff and welcome visitors. Central to the brief was the desire for the design to reflect Red Bull's involvement in sport, music and the arts.

Located in a London conservation area in Tooley Street, The Terrace was originally four separate buildings. Three of the four buildings had been linked together by the developer to create a modern space. MoreySmith connected the fourth building, and through the fit-out further joined all four buildings both visually and physically.

The character of the old building has been successfully married with the new by retaining many original features, such as large 'shop front' windows and exposed brickwork throughout. A new central staircase links the lounge and reception vertically with all office floors. Bridges and stair-links join spaces horizontally, providing connectivity across the new atrium.

The ground floor is now one large open space with sliding glass panels. The space is multi-functional and features a reception desk by day and cocktail bar for events, and at the far end of the building the Red Bull Lounge provides a space to meet, greet and entertain guests.

MoreySmith
www.moreysmith.com

Chapter 3 of this book discusses the benefits of interior design in some detail, but I would like to bring a core concept of that chapter in here – People, Planet, Profit. The Three Ps is a model that can sustain and promote meaningful design. It is about design that will really be compatible with the users' needs and will benefit the people we design for as well as the people who are involved in making and producing the design; will respect, not harm, our planet; and still be commercially viable and profitable for all involved, not just the top feeders. These three tenets should underpin all design decisions and help us as a profession to really make a difference – to people, to the planet and to profit.

It is this that separates the professional from the amateur, the meaningful from the clichéd, the lasting from the disposable.

The Toolkit

2

Overview

This chapter is intended to explore in fairly general terms the broad range of skills and knowledge that an interior designer is expected to have in their toolkit and knowledge bank. Much of this is not widely discussed or taught either at college or working in the profession, and is learnt on the job and gained over years of experience and trial and error.

This chapter is divided into four sections:

1. **Creativity and innovation.** This is not a book about the creative process. There are many books out there that explore it, but I think it is important to include an overview of the creative skills that an interior designer should have.
2. **Technicality and practicality.** Again, this is not a book to teach the practical and technical aspects of interior design. It is included here to put these skills into the context of what an interior designer is expected to understand and the knowledge they need about materials and construction. This can be partially learnt at college, but real learning and knowledge comes from working in the profession and seeing projects built on site.
3. **Communication and collaboration** looks at the collaborative nature of design, the team of people that might be involved in a project and the range of communications that need to be considered. Chapter 4: The Client-Designer Relationship expands on this and examines how to develop the special relationship in much more detail.
4. **Business and strategy** gives an overview of the broad range of knowledge and methods of working through non-design issues that arise on design projects, the philosophy and ethical stance that underpins the designer's business, running a design business, and understanding the client's business.

Creativity and innovation

Creativity in the context of interior design is not art. It is innovation and ingenuity, persistent curiosity, exploration and testing, analysis, problem identification and solving – and yes, of course, a feel for the aesthetic: colour, texture, light and atmosphere. This section looks at key creativity skills that underpin the design process:

■   **Vision** – the big picture, the space, form and volume, materials, furniture, light, colour, texture, the concept and solution to the design problem.

- **Space and form** – inserting, removing and modifying elements, scale and proportion, hierarchies of spaces and visual impact, solids and voids, organisation and circulation.
- **Detail** – multi-layered thinking where the visual language of the small details informs the overall concept and creates a visual and aesthetic continuity.
- **Function** – balancing functionality with aesthetics so they support and reinforce each other; a practical understanding allows for creative flexibility.
- **Context** – the existing building, user needs, understanding both as well as the creative challenges and constraints they create.
- **Drawing** – as a way of exploring ideas and communicating to clients and constructors – freehand, technical, digital.

Vision

The most important creative skill a designer needs to have, and hold onto, is the overall vision of the project. This means developing the creative concept from the initial client briefing by understanding and testing the client's needs and desires, analysing the existing space and context and identifying the constraints of the project/site. It requires being able to see the big picture, but also an appreciation of how the details affect the big picture, then ingeniously combining them to find a solution to the problem. This solution is ultimately the motivation for the project. The designer then needs to hold onto that vision throughout the design process.

Many unexpected and unforeseen factors will come into play at all stages of the project that will test the vision and potentially dilute it. For example, a change to the budget or timescale. These factors and the constraints and challenges that arise can often be positive factors in pushing forward the creativity of the designer. Likewise, creative compromises and adjustments are a natural part of all projects. Whatever the scenario, the designer needs to be a flexible and creative thinker who is open to change and modification, but who will also retain the essence of the concept. It will need continual lateral and creative thinking to resolve these challenges whilst at the same time balancing the vision with the agreed concept that the client expects.

There are two key creative attitudes that the designer needs in order to identify, design, develop and ultimately realise the vision of an interiors project:

1. **Visual and aesthetic.** A strong vision and feel for the appearance of the finished scheme – the materials, colour, light, furniture, balance and form, atmosphere, detail and an understanding of the impact of the design on the space and volume, balancing visual form and function.

2. **Curiosity**. Imaginative questioning at every stage to understand the purpose of the design, testing and exploring ideas, viewing constraints as exciting challenges with potentially maverick solutions, accommodating and pushing the limits of the context, ingenious planning to get the most from the space, unusual uses for mundane materials. Finally, balancing these with the visual and aesthetic.

We bring together different talents from each of our disciplines, open our minds and let our imaginations soar. We're insightful, refreshing and brave. We dream dreams – and then we build them.

Contagious, creative brand agency[1]

Brinkworth

House, Kiddepore, London, UK

Brinkworth was asked to redesign a detached five-bedroom house in a London conservation area. Despite its ample size, the interior arrangement crippled the living experience. Long corridors took spatial preference over room size and two large staircases dominated the organisation of the habitable spaces, resulting in isolated rooms and a lack of natural light. Consequently, the house suffered from inefficient lighting and heating solutions typical of a 1930s period house.

The clients envisioned the project changing the space of the house in order to utilise it properly – both visually and architecturally – as well as keeping design features as minimal as possible. Brinkworth's strategy was to excavate what was not needed, rationalise each floor level and service these with a single staircase of steel and concrete, eliminating wasteful corridors.

Kevin Brennan from Brinkworth explained: 'We were aware that our intentions would be fairly invasive, but we were sensitive to our intervention as guests and the existing envelope being a very accommodating host to our occupation, taking advantage of possibilities without losing the rhythm of the house.'

The clients required only a basic level of accommodation, which gave enough slack to create an impressive void. To find this volume the first floor plate was removed, leaving a double height box of 10m × 10m × 10m.

The overall design focuses on a 'box within a box' concept (inspired by conceptual artist Dan Graham's work with transparency and reflection) incorporating the isolation of different living space areas. A mezzanine, a new back extension, cubes that resourcefully double-up as furniture and smaller corridors all inform one another without physical contact, maintaining an optimum fluidity of space.

The kitchen, also part of the living room area, continues this concealed concept; all the utilities are hidden away in blocks until the space needs to be used, enabling the client to alternate between the two separate environments. The garden was levelled and re-landscaped to immerse it further into the design scheme of the house.

The intimacy of the house has been retained through the use of exposed natural materials. There are Douglas Fir lime-washed broad planks throughout the ground floor, whilst black oak is used on the mezzanine, in harmony with the extension ceiling parallel to it, emphasising the overall warmth in design.

Brinkworth
www.brinkworth.co.uk

Space and form

Simplistically, an appreciation of space and form is what differentiates an interior designer from an interior decorator. Appreciation of space and form can include:

- scale and proportion
- hierarchies of spaces and visual weight
- voids and solids
- organisation and circulation.

Understanding the existing building (or the new building in some cases), its volume and how it might be spatially altered by inserting, removing and modifying architectural elements to obtain the maximum desired effect and usable space is the fundamental skill of an interior designer. A stylist or decorator is usually more concerned with choosing, placing and combining surface treatments, furniture, fixtures and equipment. Of course there is no absolute dividing line between the two, and the designer must be skilled in decorative finishes, but it is important that the designer informs the client of their specialism and limits, so that there is no misunderstanding by the former of the latter's ability or experience. If the project requires extensive architectural redesign or structural changes, it is essential to collaborate with an architect or structural engineer to meet Professional Indemnity insurance requirements.

When in a space, we do not think of ourselves moving about a two-dimensional plan drawing; we appreciate (often subconsciously) the three-dimensional qualities of it: the volume, the size and height of the space, how it is used, and where furniture and walls are placed in order to contain the space, to direct us through it and to give us glimpses into another space. We have emotional and physical responses to the design, the quality of light, the materials, the colour, the texture, the juxtaposition of new against old, the generous height of the space or deliberately cropped view to the world outside. Understanding how we respond to interior spaces, and how spaces can be manipulated to achieve specific desired affects on the user, are the most fundamental skills an interior designer should have.

... these primary elements of form and space comprise the timeless and fundamental vocabulary of the architectural designer.

Francis D.K. Ching[2]

Detail

Generating the initial visual concept is often thought of as the fun bit, but it takes a great deal of consistent effort to retain the essence of the concept through to the finished interior. To develop the concept and make it real and tangible, a multi-layered approach of thinking is needed from the very big picture to the most minuscule detail.

Where in the design process does this attention to detail come in? Towards the end, near the actual build? Yes, but also crucially it should be a part of the initial concept discussion, as it will sustain a consistent 'design language' throughout the project, which will impact on the visual aesthetic and the budget. There are two aspects to working in detail:

1. The **visual language** of the detail is an essential component of the concept and requires general decisions to be taken early on about the level of decoration in the details and, depending on the concept, whether they echo or contrast the age and style of the building. It must match the vision.
2. A **practical understanding** of detail design. Consideration of the technical, and their financial implications, is essential. For example, at its most simplistic, minimal detailing can be more expensive than decorative detailing, as joints and junctions are not covered with a decorative element and have to be constructed to a higher quality, possibly requiring specialist trades.

This multi-layered level of thinking about detail requires the designer to have an understanding of how things go together – joints and junctions, visible or invisible fixings, what materials can and cannot do, how to use everyday materials in an innovative way or situation. Without this skill, the finished project is likely to be a compromised version of the original concept.

Is attention to detail a technical aspect? Yes, but it is more crucially a creative one, as it requires an ability to approach the challenges of detail design with an attitude of exploration and invention – it adds depth to the concept and vision. A good design is one that has challenged the limitations of the project (space, budget, expectations) and used all the resources, down to the last screw head, to their maximum potential.

Function

Is it fit for purpose? Does it work? Is it practical? Does its appearance fit with the concept?

Perhaps not immediately an obvious creative skill, function relates back to detail thinking and the fact that the designer needs to be able to balance functionality with aesthetics. Does form follow function, is it equal to function, or does function follow form? All three variations are relevant depending on the circumstance, the problem, the brief and the constraints.

Function relates to two key aspects of interior design:

1. **What the space is made of, and how it is constructed, including:**
    - **Materials** – understanding their inherent qualities and capabilities. The ability to decide where and how to use them, or how to use them in unusual or unexpected situations.
    - **Construction** – understanding material capabilities allows the designer to be creative about how and where they are used, as well as the specific construction methods employed.
2. **How people occupy the space and move around it, including:**
    - **Planning** – to really utilise the full potential of the space in a way that is true to the original concept by ingenious arrangement of spaces and contents which fufils the needs of the users and the client.
    - **Circulation** – moving around and between spaces, minimising areas used for circulation, creating ease of movement without unnecessary obstructions, cleverly getting people to move through the space in a particular way, or to encourage healthy activity.

Clients will always comment if something in the finished scheme is not working well. It may look amazing, but if one small element breaks down, wears badly or feels uncomfortable, it could easily be a niggling problem that may overshadow the whole project. Likewise if the scheme, or a part of it, does not fulfil the intent of commercial clients for their business needs and efficiency.

From the smallest detail to the circulation and planning of a space, it is the interior designer's job to balance the functional and practical requirements with the concept and vision. A good knowledge bank of the practical potential and limits of an object, a volume, a material, means that their limits can be pushed and reshaped. This knowledge allows the functional requirements to support and inform conceptual and aesthetic design decisions, whilst knowing that the proposal is feasible, fit for purpose and will suit the budget and its user needs.

We believe that good things not only
look great but are designed to work.

Rachel Forster, Forster Inc [3]

Context

An interior designer will nearly always be working within an existing building (or working with architects to design interiors for a new build), always with a client, and usually with a group of users with specific needs. Therefore we need to make it our business to understand the architecture, history and social anthropology related to the building and the people involved in the project – the context.

Understanding the context informs the creative process. Like most aspects of interior design, it is about balance between lateral analytical thinking and using the outcomes of that thinking in innovative and creative ways to bring the brief to life.

At the earliest stage of a project, the architectural context needs to be analysed and understood in order to ascertain whether it is possible to fulfil the client's brief, if it fits their purpose in terms of its general suitability for the client's needs, the viability of any structural alterations if required, and what value and benefits these alterations will offer the client and end users. Interior designers also need to be aware of the constraints that might be imposed by regulations, site/size limitations, and whether there is enough money in the budget to warrant the re-use of this building – that is, the balance of benefit to cost. It is also important to understand the age and history of the building, in order to decide which parts need to be retained, what can be taken away and whether there are any planning restrictions or heritage issues.

Interior designers are re-users of buildings[4] (with the obvious exception of working on a new build); we up-cycle them, we renovate, restore and adapt them, we cherish the context we have been asked to work with. However, this does not mean we must create a pastiche interior to try to copy the context. It may be that to really appreciate the building, a totally opposite architectural design language is chosen to create drama and tension – or to allow the existing context to 'breathe' by not overpowering it with complex spatial interventions. This is where the creative skill comes into play and can only be successful if the designer has a full understanding of the context.

The existing context, structure, spaces, function and history can offer many significant conceptual opportunities and an appreciation and interpretation of these can provide the inspiration for the redesign.

Graeme Brooker and Sally Stone[5]

Drawing

Drawing, in the context of interior design is for two purposes:

1. to explore and develop ideas visually, and
2. to communicate the design to others.

The drawing is not the end product, it is not a work of art; it is a means of realising an interior design. It is a two-dimensional way of communicating the information that is needed to build the three-dimensional interior. The method of drawing is obviously down to the skill and choice of the designer.

Drawing, at first speculatively and then precisely to scale, is the means to test most rigorously how a near-abstract concept can be viably translated into reality.

Drew Plunkett[6]

Whether hand-drawn or computer-generated, drawings need to be:

- useful to the designer as a way of exploring ideas and recording the development of the design
- legible
- appropriate to those who will view them. For instance, most clients do not understand construction, so this level of information would not be appropriate in presentation drawings
- appropriate to the stage of the project. For instance, very technically detailed drawings before the client has signed off the concept could mean a lot of time spent for no return if the client does not approve
- a dated, numbered record of the project in case of a dispute.

Sketch drawings

The computer is an amazing drawing tool, but if a designer can draw and sketch freehand, they will be able to really explore and develop ideas quickly, inventively and intuitively. Sketches are used to develop and explore design ideas and the concept. They are a way of thinking, a way of visually representing internal conversations about design decisions – it is about taking a line for a walk in order to explore an idea. Sketches collated into a sketchbook along with notes and images are a fabulous record of the development of a project, for both the designer and the client to appreciate just how much thought, time and development goes into a project and to demonstrate that many options have been considered. They are also very human and tactile, frequently becoming cherished items. Sketch drawings are often used extensively at the beginning of a project, to get ideas going and to explore them. But they are also a great tool for use throughout a project for working out details and junctions and for explaining visually something to clients, who love it when designers draw what they are talking about during meetings.

A sketchbook to record travels, buildings, details – a visual notebook – is invaluable as a way of really looking, seeing, understanding and recording the built environment, and as a serial sketcher myself I encourage all designers to get into the habit of sketching.

We do a significant amount of freehand drawing for initial proposals as clients understand them, they are more personal than computer drawings

Rachel Bowyer, Director of New Business Development, Brinkworth.[7]

Digital drawings

Most students are introduced to computer drawing skills very early on in their training nowadays, and so are very accomplished users. However, the interiors profession took a little time to catch up with architecture practices which embraced computer drawings from the very beginning. The problem for designers was that many software packages for digital drawings were incredibly expensive – too much for a very small practice to carry. However, the cost has reduced dramatically, and the time-saving that an interiors practice can benefit from by using computer drawings can help to offset the high capital costs of equipment and software.

As a general principle, computer drawings are used when the initial design ideas have been established, when there is sufficient information to be translated into a workable plan, section or 3D view. However, there are designers and architects whose work is driven by digital technology to generate ideas and concepts and who would not be able to design, make their structures work, or build their amazing constructions without it – for example, works by Zaha Hadid Architects, or the Bird's Nest stadium in Beijing by Herzog de Meuron and artist Ai Weiwei.

As software programmes become more and more sophisticated, the use of computers at all stages of the design process will be more prevalent. Importantly, Building Information Modelling (BIM) is playing a huge part in how digital work is used in the design of interiors and buildings. This is where the scheme is modelled totally in digital format. The information included is incredibly specific, down to the smallest details (which can be imported from the manufacturer's BIM digital library). This information in turn can generate specification information, schedules, costings and so on, so that any changes made to the design are immediately changed on all the relevant drawings and documentation. It is then a total package of digital information that is accessible to the whole project team for the duration of the project, making collaboration easier, reducing misunderstandings, and which then stays with the interior or building for future clients and designers to have access to. This makes the whole design process more transparent and accessible to future designers. Again, architects are increasingly using BIM widely in practice – as of April 2016 BIM has been a requirement for all public sector work. Interior designers have been slower to pick it up – probably due to the cost of the software and the smaller scope of their projects. This is likely to change, with software companies offering interior designers 'light' versions of the heavyweight architecture packages.

Technical drawings

These types of drawings can be divided into two key types that are specific to the concept design and production – or technical – design (see Chapter 4 for more information on design stages):

1. **Presentation drawings** – to present and sell the initial concept to the client. These are usually in the form of plans, sections and 3D views to give the client an overall vision of the scheme. Plans will show general spatial and furniture layout, sections will present an overall feel for the design language that is being used, and are often rendered to give a feel for colour and materials. 3D views might be sketched and hand-rendered, or computer-generated, and illustrate materials, colour and lighting. They are aimed at 'selling' the project, so will be as atmospheric as possible to show the client how the finished interior might look. As a lot of clients are not used to looking at drawings, many designers integrate quite a bit of freehand drawing at this stage to help clients feel comfortable.

2. **Production** – to finalise detail design that can be sent out to contractors for costing and executing the build. These drawings are inherently different to presentation drawings as they are specifically for contractors and specialist suppliers who need accurate, measured and detailed information in order to carefully cost and execute the build. A comprehensive and detailed set of production drawings can help to avoid budget overspend, sub-standard build quality and inappropriate use of materials, all of which could lead to client dissatisfaction. Specialist and bespoke contractors often issue their own production drawings based on the designer's schematic drawings. Production drawings are generally digitally produced, which makes for ease of communication with contractors, suppliers and users. This digital record can then be collated as part of a BIM package, if required.

Drawing

As Drew Plunkett, architect and interior designer, says, 'drawing, at first speculatively and then precisely to scale, is the means to test most rigorously how a near-abstract concept can be viably translated into reality.'

Conversely, drawing is also an essential tool for the designer as a means of examining and exploring our existing realities to inform near-abstract concepts and design ideas.

Drawing architecture, interiors, furniture, details, pattern, texture, light, shadows and so on from life builds a subliminal filing cabinet to draw on for design ideas and solutions. Drawing from life requires deeper looking and analysis than photography, which is fleeting and captures a moment; a drawing can capture a sense of place that will also evoke the sounds and smells of that place. And a sketchbook of drawings captures a life of looking and experiencing our world around us. For more inspiration take a look at Urban Sketchers – a community of people of all artistic abilities (many of whom are artists, architects and designers) from all around the world who 'show the world one drawing at a time'.

 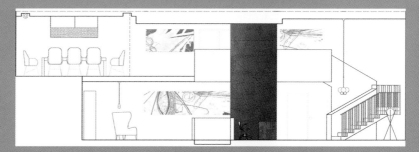

The drawings illustrated here show a small selection of work by interior design students, practising designers and artists – from a quick sketch to understand the bizarre layout of a restaurant in Fez, Morocco and the route to its toilet, to computer-rendered 3D views and sketches to explore the design of a staircase. They just touch on the vast world of drawing techniques, tools and points of view which all designers should explore and embrace.

Drawing is how we think and make decisions. By taking a line on a journey we will discover ourselves, our design philosophies, and enable us to communicate often ethereal concepts to our clients.

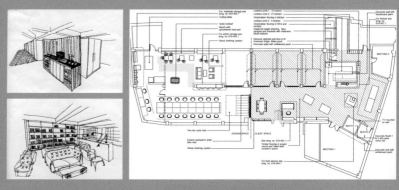

MEETING ROOM

RECEPTION

MAIN ENTRANCE

WAITING AREA

COFFE BAR / MEETING ROOM

COURT YARD

Technicality and practicality

We have established that creativity and innovation are the motivating forces that drive a project. Underpinning these skills, the designer needs to have a fundamental expertise in technical and practical issues in order to get the project built; to make it tangible and real.

The designer needs to have a good general level of knowledge and understanding of the technical scope of their design, but it would be impossible to be an expert in all these areas:

- **Materials** – what it is made of.
- **FF+E** – furniture, fixtures and equipment.
- **Construction and detailing** – structure, junctions, corners, fixings, how things are made.
- **Environmental and building services** – plumbing, electrics, communications, media, IT, energy conservation.
- **Regulations** – building, heritage, safety, planning, sustainability.

Advanced technical expertise comes with experience, but most designers will usually pull together a team of specialists, appointed independently by the client. The skill is in knowing who needs to be brought on board in order for the whole vision to be realised.

Materials

Selecting materials is an obvious example of striving for the balance between creativity and practicality. In the early stages of concept, deciding a 'palette' of colour, texture and visual weight is essential. The technical expertise comes at the concept and feasibility stages, in identifying the materials best suited to the context whilst satisfying the creative vision and budget.

As we have already seen, the designer's job is to balance the aesthetic with the practical. This is equally true when thinking about materials. Here are some things to consider:

- Are the materials durable enough for the degree of expected use?
- Does the finished appearance of the material and how it is detailed (i.e. how it meets another material, turns a corner, is fixed) justify very skilled and expensive labour and installation costs?
- Is weight a factor? For instance, a stone kitchen counter might need a reinforced floor to carry the additional weight, the cost of which will impact on the budget.

- Accessibility – how to get large pieces of material into the building, for example glass and sheet materials.
- When to compromise the visual impact of a material for the sake of durability and longevity – and vice versa – and the effect the decision has on the budget.
- The power of using a very 'normal' material in unexpected ways or amounts, for example exterior grade chipboard being used as an interior wall finish.

The designer needs to continually adapt their own knowledge of materials through research, observation of how they have been used by others, and Continuing Professional Development (CPD) talks.[8]

Every material should only be used after careful consideration of its environmental impact (see Chapter 3, pp. 93–95, for further discussion on this issue):

- the use of natural resources
- the manufacturing method and the working conditions of the makers
- the method of shipping and country of origin
- understanding standard sizes of materials and designing and, with that knowledge in mind, reducing waste.

Interior design, by its very nature, is potentially an extremely wasteful business. Fashion and trends can tend to dictate and lead to interiors being ripped out with all the attendant waste that results. We need to design with attention to all of this in order to keep to a minimum the harmful environmental impact of our work.[9]

Furniture, fixtures and equipment (FF+E)

In a similar way to the use of materials, the selection of furniture, fixtures and equipment has a very creative aspect to it as these elements have to work within the overall vision and concept. But this visual aesthetic needs to be balanced with the amount of wear and tear they can withstand, functionality, suitability to purpose, and fire and safety issues. The designer needs to make educated choices that consider all of these technical aspects.

Items that are used daily and touched often should be carefully chosen because if they do not work, wear quickly or fail in any other technical or functional aspect, the client will be unhappy. It is often these seemingly small things that can distract the client's appreciation from the whole interior.

As with materials, sustainability is a huge issue here. Even though much has changed in the last few years, interior design seems destined to be inextricably linked with a disposable mentality. As designers, we have a moral and ethical responsibility to encourage our clients to take environmental issues seriously, so that selection of FF+E is based on sustainability, longevity and, wherever possible, re-use.

FF+E comes from two main sources:

1.   commercial suppliers or
2.   bespoke makers.

Working with a craftsman is a collaboration and their technical expertise feeds into the design of the piece. Sourcing from a commercial supplier is more of a consumer experience: buying the right thing for the right price. Many designers develop long relationships with craftsmen and suppliers, which can be beneficial to the client because the designer knows the product, how it has performed on other projects, and will guide the client with regard to what they can expect in terms of quality of workmanship or manufacture. They may also be able to negotiate a discount in cost on behalf of the client. See Chapter 4, p. 123 and p. 128, regarding the often contentious issue of designer discounts for FF+E.

Construction and detailing

In order to develop an initial concept, the designer needs to understand basic structural and construction principles so that they recognise how their design choices and decisions will impact on their own design fee, as well as the construction costs and deadlines of the project. Construction can mean the 'big' interior elements – for example, methods for constructing a wall, new floors or ceilings. But it also means construction right down to the tiniest details of how a shelf is held up, or the junction between two different wall materials. All will require a similar attitude of thought and all require the same questions to be asked. For example, how is one material joined to another? How is it supported? What will the junctions look like? Will the fixings be visible or hidden?

On projects in an existing building, rather than a new build, where major remodelling is envisaged and new architectural interventions are being considered (for example, removing walls or creating openings), the designer needs to have a basic understanding of what effect this might have on the existing structure and how that will impact on other areas of the design, possibly compromising the budget and the timescale. The designer should ask themselves what needs to be retained not just for structural integrity but also to maintain an aesthetic integrity that respects the history of the building. A structural engineer or architect should always be engaged by the client, on the advice of the designer, when making these types of alterations.

As Diana and Stephen Yakeley state very clearly in their book, *The BIID Interior Design Job Book*, the designer should 'never contract to provide services for which he/she is not qualified.'[10]

When designing new elements and insertions, a major early consideration is what language of construction detailing (i.e. junctions of materials, corners, visible or invisible fixings) is appropriate to the concept and the overall visual appearance of details. This detailing needs to be consistent throughout the project and is developed as part of the original concept.

The aesthetic choice of how much fixing you see holding things together (i.e. using invisible or visible fixings) generally makes a big difference in the method of construction, and inevitably means some sort of financial consequence. For example, invisible fixings generally require more of the designer's time to design the ingenious detail and prepare drawings (which the designer should accommodate in the design fee), sourcing or having specialist fixings made (bespoke is generally more expensive than commercially manufactured), and can be more time-consuming to install or require a specialist installer (labour costs).

Junctions and corners of elements and materials and how these materials meet is another key early conceptual decision. Should joints be expressed or concealed? An everyday example is doors – to architrave or not? The architrave is there to hide the inevitable gap that occurs between a junction of plaster wall finish and timber doorframe - the gap being created by the uncontrollable differences in how the materials react to changes in moisture and temperature. The traditional (and probably cheapest) form of handling this is to cover it with an architrave. The minimal approach requires a different method of construction which, depending what visual appearance is desired, might require specialist trades and construction components, and have similar consequences as using invisible fixings.

The key point to take on is that conceptual decisions need to be underpinned by a basic understanding of construction methods, structure and material capability. Without these, the designer can easily propose whimsical schemes that will raise the expectations of the client to an unattainable level. If in doubt, consult a relevant engineer, specialist or architect to advise and help design the construction of the project to an appropriate level of detail and finish to suit the budget.

Good interior detailing is bespoke, an informed response not only to the practical demands of a new interior but also to the physical characteristics of the existing structure that will enclose it.

Drew Plunkett.[11]

Environmental and building services

We are considering here how services are designed into the scheme, rather than their building and installation. As previously discussed, designers are great generalists; they tend to have good all-round knowledge, but this is one part of their work where they may well need technical advice and specialist knowledge on:

- plumbing
- lighting
- electrics
- electronics and digital
- acoustics and sound
- heating, ventilation and air handling
- the environmental impact of energy consumption.

Having said that, a basic understanding of all of these is essential for the designer. When pulling together an initial proposal it would be a nonsense if the designer planned a new bathroom too far away from existing drainage points for it to be feasible, or does not understand the structural constraint of specifying recessed lighting in a solid ceiling.

The designer needs to explain to their client just how specialised designing services into an interior is and that, depending on the complexity of the project, consultants might need to be part of the team – for example, a digital services designer to integrate media systems into a home. Because of the regulatory nature and technical/scientific expertise required to design many of these services, the designer must never design without definitive knowledge in these areas. If in the slightest doubt, specialist advice should be taken to ensure the designer is not liable if there are problems later down line, as their liability insurance is unlikely to cover them.

Continual technological advances in control systems for services and the impact this has – particularly on media and communication systems – makes for an interesting challenge for the designer to integrate into a design. Specialist designers and engineers will be essential on any project that has computerised digital systems. For example, a company reception area that has a digital wall displaying information about the company – perhaps interactive – showing films, with sound, and lighting specific to the digital wall, or a computerised lighting system that changes the colour/levels of light depending on the activity in the space, or time of day, or atmosphere desired.

Plumbing is a general term covering a huge amount of works – hot and cold water installations, drainage and soil waste systems, gas- and oil-fired hot water circulating central heating installations, grey water collection and use. It generally needs to conform to building standards for health and safety to ensure there is no contamination to drinking water supplies or pollution to the environment.[12] Depending on the size and scope of the project, a suitably well-qualified plumber will be able to address most issues. On larger or more complex projects, a specialist will be required to advise.

Lighting has a massive impact on the atmosphere of a space. Understanding what natural and artificial light does and how to manipulate it requires technical expertise that, depending on the size of the project, can be beyond the designer's experience. However, the designer should know the atmosphere they are trying to create, then use a specialist to design and specify it. Consulting either a specialist independent lighting designer or an in-house designer of a large manufacturer or supplier is usually the best way forward. The digital control systems that are prevalent now require not only design expertise but may also require specialist installation experts. This all needs to be factored into the consultancy fees that the client might need to pay. All lighting installations should now endeavour to reduce energy consumption as much as possible.[13]

Electrics can range from simple residential re-wiring and electrical installations to the installation of complex heat-exchange heating systems to specialist commercial fit-outs requiring integrated communications and media installations and digital control systems. The range of specialists is broad and the designer should identify to the client if a specialist consultant is needed to design and supervise the installation of this work.

Electronics and digital includes areas such as communications and computer networks, TV/film, sound, lighting and heating controls. The advances in these areas happen almost on a daily basis and are impossible to keep up with unless you are a techno-geek. However, designers should be curious about developments in these fields, as they are opening up new and exciting ways of designing, building and maintaining interiors. A good starting point for research and staying up to speed is *Installation International*, an online magazine offering global news and articles on new technology and advances in this field.[14]

Acoustics and sound for sound quality, to reduce the impact of sound pollution and for designing environments such as nightclubs, cinemas and theatres.

Heating, ventilation and air handling – the options for handling heating and air handling are often limited by the existing context (the building and structural constraints) or the supply of available energy resources. There is a huge amount of research into these aspects of the built environment as they are one of the major consumers of energy and we all have a role to play in reducing consumption as much as possible. Heating by solar, heat pumps, or no heating at all thanks to high insulation levels and methods of construction, are becoming more popular and affordable. However, these are often easier to install in new builds than in existing buildings, so the constraints imposed by the building and cost will factor into the equation. For these reasons, if a major overhaul of these services is required, a specialist is a good idea to balance out the pros and cons of possible routes against the short- and long-term benefits. Clients are now much more knowledgeable about the environmental choices open to them and designers should encourage them to support a design that is designed and built in the most energy-efficient way possible.[15]

The environment and impact of energy consumption. There is an environmental impact to be considered when designing and integrating any services into a design scheme. All energy consuming elements must be carefully considered for their environmental impact in terms of energy efficiency, production method and impact on pollution, and longevity of the product. With strict regulations being regularly updated it is crucial that designers are aware of what they can and should do versus what they cannot and should not do. Two globally recognised certification methods that promote, support and rate sustainable design are BREEAM and SEED, and both have available a great deal of information and resources for designers.[16]

Regulations

Regulations are obviously determined by the location of the project, and vary hugely from country to country depending on attitudes to health, safety, disability, environment and heritage. The UK has very complex and comprehensive regulations for the construction industry, all requiring consideration by the designer during the early stages of the design process, as they will impact on decisions and some will require early official consents. They can be grouped together schematically into three areas for consideration:

1. **Feasibility and design** – planning regulations, building regulations, conservation, party wall.
2. **Construction** – health and safety of the people working on the construction and site, and of the design, structure, materials and processes used in building the scheme. This is particularly onerous in the UK, which has **Construction (Design and Management) Regulations (CDM)** that apply to all construction projects including domestic. The designer, client and contractor all have duties to fulfil under these regulations and must be absolutely sure of their role and responsibilities on a project to ensure this set of regulations is complied with.[17] A useful resource for members of the BIID is access to a CDM Helpline, available through the BIID website.
3. **Occupation** – health, safety and accessibility of the occupants, fire, electrics, air quality, disabled access.

These three key areas are a simplistic global model for all designers to consider so that their interiors conform to their country's regulations and legislation or, where none exist, they are working to a high level of responsible design to protect:

- the heritage of the building
- the health and safety of the people building the scheme
- the environmental and structural integrity of the materials and processes used to build the scheme
- the health, safety and accessibility of the occupants.

It is impossible for the designer to have a comprehensive knowledge of all relevant regulations. However, it is crucial that they are aware of which regulations might be applicable to the project, who the authorities are, when to contact them and who should contact them. There are often several routes in choosing who needs to be involved in a project. For example to comply with Building Regulations in the UK, approval for certain works is required and can be granted either by the Local Authority, or by a private Approved Inspector, or even by a building contractor who is registered to self-certify some of the work they are undertaking. It is the designer's job to ensure that all involved in the project understand their responsibilities.[18] It is often good practice to contact the relevant officials early in a project, as their knowledge and collaboration can be incredibly useful during the design process and should smooth through any required approvals.

Communication and collaboration

From looking at the results of the case study interviews conducted by the author,[19] good communication is the clear leader in achieving a successful project and to winning repeat business. A design project is always a collaboration between people with specialist skills, expertise and knowledge, and is most successful when everyone knows their role and responsibilities. Grey areas are avoided and work is not missed or repeated, which, in turn, should positively impact on budget and timescale.

The designer needs to lead and drive the project, keeping an eye on all aspects of it, but also needs a team of people to help and collaborate through transparent, frequent, honest and documented communications:

- ■ **Spoken** – meetings, informal discussions through telephone calls or face-to-face
- ■ **Written** – letters, emails, reports, meeting notes, schedules, instructions, contracts and agreements
- ■ **Visual** – drawings, models, samples.

This section identifies the key people and teams involved in a project; their roles and responsibilities and the consequences of good and bad communications.

Pick up the phone if there is
a problem, instead of an email.
Do what you say you will do.

Jason Milne, Creative Director Environments, Contagious[20]

Communications

To reiterate: to have happy clients, teams and successful projects, everyone must communicate to identify and explain who does what, when they do it, how they do it, and address problems as soon as they arise. Disputes often occur because of a breakdown in communications, so the whole team is responsible for working together to avoid such a scenario. These communications should always be:

- ■ frequent
- ■ honest
- ■ relevant
- ■ respectful
- ■ trusting
- ■ documented.

It is the designer's duty to explain very clearly to the client just what is involved in their project, and exactly what will be required of them. First-time clients often do not understand the extensive process and number of consultants that may be needed in creating an interior, so quite a lot of explanation and hand-holding is often involved. Even if the client has worked with the designer previously, there will still be a need for the designer to explain the specific issues relating to the current project.

A professional, honest and respectful approach to communicating with the design, construction and regulatory teams will build strong foundations for a successful business for the designer.

The client

The client, or key decision-maker, is top of the list of people with whom to establish a clear and easy line of communication and the client should be made aware from the outset just how important their role is in creating an environment that fulfils, or exceeds, their expectations.

At the briefing stage, the client may not know exactly what they want or need, so the designer's task is to spend time talking to them, digging deep and questioning, exploring and discovering the motivations that are driving the project. It is this open, creative relationship that is most likely to produce distinctive projects, and is a significant part of the design process.

Forster Inc

IDEO, White Bear Yard, Clerkenwell, London, UK

When IDEO, the design and innovation consulting firm, approached Forster Inc to refurbish its existing London studio, it was looking for a team to design a scheme that not only looked great and embodied its brand values but fulfilled its various styles of working. IDEO wanted a creative, non-corporate environment that could accommodate client and internal meetings, individual and group working, eating, drinking, having fun and that it could be proud of. IDEO's approach is creative, accessible and collaborative, where multidisciplinary teams work closely with clients in long-term relationships, but on a project-by-project basis, often taking clients away from their more typical office spaces to help drive creativity and innovation.

The existing industrial warehouse building is the backdrop into which domestic and café culture references were introduced. Texture from the chosen materials and the layout create a welcoming, homely space where communal spaces are both functional and social, creating the buzz of a coffee shop but always enabling the day-to-day work life in the studio.

The design process was collaborative from the start and this collaboration was instrumental to the success of the project. Rachel Forster and her team asked each employee to complete a questionnaire on the current office, the company, their likes and dislikes, and how they wanted to be perceived. The responses formed the basis of the design and everyone felt listened to and engaged with the process of change. The layout was rearranged to increase both private working and communal spaces that could be enjoyed as a group or individually. The kitchen and the new coffee bar have become places where serendipitous meetings take place, ideas spark, and conversations flow.

Warehouse references with engineering inspired the mix of bespoke and standard furniture. The family of three different sized oak-top bespoke tables enables single, pair and group working. The flexible shelving system from Vitsoe with Chesterfield sofa from John Lewis and armchairs from Andy Thornton enable areas to be moved around. The large reception table creates another place to work alongside a curated display of IDEO's work.

The build took just 13 days to complete on a fixed budget. The budget constraints meant the refurbishment was an opportunity for IDEO to create new space, keep what was relevant, discard what was not and introduce what was right.

The combination of café culture, the domestic and the industrial warehouse creates a comfortable, non-intrusive interior for creative and collaborative work where clients feel at ease and employees feel comfortable. This is a space where true ideas spark.

Forster Inc
www.forsterinc.co.uk

However, the client may not always be the end user, so it is important to remember that the building users may need to be a part of these initial discussions, as they might perceive the problem totally differently.

The designer should carefully explain to the client what their role is, and that any communication the client wants to have with other members of the team should always come through the designer or project manager. For example, the client issuing spoken instructions to contractors without the designer's knowledge must be avoided at all costs! It is like any major relationship that, in order to be successful, needs to have strong foundations of trust and respect. Clear boundaries, roles and responsibilities should be established at the very earliest.

It might be necessary to use different forms of communication, depending on the client type. The designer needs to gauge how best to build the relationship with the appropriate level of formality. The client is not the designer's best friend. This is a business relationship which can be informal and friendly, but there may easily come a point in the project where the relationship is put under stress and will need to be handled in a calm and professional way. It is for this reason that a formal client-designer agreement should be drawn up at the start of all projects. Chapter 4 covers this in detail.

To avoid unforeseen problems, it is not unreasonable for both client and designer to carry out some basic research on each other before the project starts – for example, a credit check and reputation check. This relationship has to feel right – trust your instincts.

There has to be chemistry.

Rachel Bowyer, Associate Director New Project Development, Brinkworth[21]

What makes a successful project? 'A client who truly values the designer's skills, and a designer who can work in a collaborative way with the client.'

Lori Pinkerton-Rolet, Park Grove Design[22]

The designer

The designer is responsible for the overall vision and integrity of the project, and the client needs to understand exactly which services the designer is performing in order to do this. It is the designer's role to collaborate with the client from the outset to bring the project to life. To do this, the designer is the pivot of communications and interpreter between the client, the design team, the consultants and the construction team, and needs to establish clear and direct lines of communication with everyone involved to avoid problems. The designer also needs to document the communications to have a complete record in case of disputes or misunderstandings.

For the purposes of this book it is assumed that the designer is the design team leader (or lead consultant) responsible for coordinating the services and work of the other consultants that form the design team, rather than a more junior designer working as part of a design team but not leading the project. However, as mentioned below, the team might be constructed differently, but the principles discussed here are equally relevant to all designers. For example, on a large architectural project the lead consultant might be an architect and the designer is working as a consultant to them. If this is the case, the designer will likely have their own team of designers and consultants working on the project, so is therefore a design team leader of that part of the project but this will be secondary to the lead consultant (i.e. the architect in this example).

Essentially, the designer's services[23] can be broken into three key areas, of which all might be required by the client, or sometimes the designer works as a consultant or advisor on individual areas:

1. **Design** – from briefing, feasibility and concept through to detail and production drawings.
2. **Building** – the designer acting as either the main contractor (has own building team) or supervising the contract that the client has entered into with a third-party main contractor.
3. **FF+E** – the designer acts either as agent or principal in sourcing and/or supplying furniture, fixtures and equipment. Acting as an agent means the designer is advising the client on which FF+E to buy. Acting as a principal means the designer is selling FF+E directly to the client. It is important that the client understands this difference, and how they will be charged in each instance.

Time spent by the designer explaining, discussing and documenting their role and responsibilities with the client will prove invaluable during the course of the project, to avoid the latter having unreasonable expectations of the services the former will provide. The designer should never assume that the client understands what processes are involved in designing and executing a project, so a very thorough Schedule of Design Services should be provided to the client.[24] Chapter 4 discusses this in more detail.

The design team

The design team is as large or as small as the project demands. The overall aim is to take a collaborative approach and use each other's knowledge and skills.

The team described below is the basic pool of expertise that the designer should be able to call on if the project requires it. The designer must never take on responsibility for an area of the work they are not qualified to do, so should discuss this with the client at the outset and decide which expert consultants should be appointed. Although it will be the designer communicating with these consultants, they are doing so on behalf of the client, and it is the client who will appoint them – not the designer. Larger design companies may have some members of the design team working in-house who will be included in the overall design fee. If not, and they are appointed by the client, they will bill the client directly for their work.

We have already looked at the key roles of the client and the designer. The other important members of the design team that might need to be engaged are:

- **Architect** – if major architectural alterations or insertions are required. On a large project, or where the interior is in a new build, the architect may well be the design team leader.
- **Quantity surveyor** – to prepare initial cost estimates, monitor the building contract tender and procurement processes, facilitate the client/contractor contract, monitor costs and the budget throughout the building contract. The QS acts very much on the client's behalf to balance value for money against achieving the desired and required design standards.
- **Structural engineer** – advises on structural changes to the existing building, calculates structural specifications for components to be supplied/installed by the main contractor, submits calculations to the building control surveyor for approval.
- **Surveyor** – offers a wide range of general building and construction advice and can be a valuable asset to a design team.
- **Lighting designer** – an increasingly complex and specialist field of work requiring in-depth knowledge of technical and computerised systems and environmental standards.
- **Mechanical, electrical, services, environment, systems engineers** – advise and provide specifications for heating, ventilation, air handling, electrical and computerised control systems, environmental issues; oversee these works on site; are knowledgeable about sustainability, regulations and renewable energy sources.
- **IT, computer, media services specialist** – the technology and digital experts that are becoming more and more important as technology gets more complex.
- **Suppliers of FF+E** – specialist installation knowledge and appropriateness to scheme.
- **Specialist designers/suppliers** – for example, for kitchens and bathrooms.
- **Bespoke makers/craftspeople** – designers should learn from them and work creatively with them.
- **Graphic designer** – to advise on and design brand and identity (commercial schemes).
- **3D visualisers** – digital perspectives and walk-throughs of proposed schemes.

Construction team

Depending on the size and scope of the project, there are basically two main ways of appointing a construction team:[25]

1. Designers using their in-house or preferred building contractor(s) to negotiate a price and timescale.

2. Third-party contractors selected from a formal tender process to obtain a competitive price which is balanced with quality and attention to detail and timescale.

There are advantages and disadvantages to both routes. The advantages to using the designer's in-house or preferred contractors are that the designer and contractor are often used to working with each other, have good existing communication methods and have developed a kind of shorthand in their relationship. The disadvantage is that the client may feel they are not getting value for money without a contract tender process. Having a quantity surveyor on the team should mean that whichever route is taken, the client is getting value for money for the desired quality of the build. The quantity surveyor is a key member of the team, as they are able to advise on the most suitable form of construction contract to be used that will ensure fairness and efficiency – for example, lump sum, cost plus fixed fee, design & build contracts. They will also be able to advise on the various procurement routes, and then manage and report on the tendering and negotiation processes to select contractors.

There are essentially two main ways of managing a building project and the people who are going to do this need to be identified as early as possible. They will establish how the building works are scheduled and managed so that everything happens in the necessary sequence during the build:

1. **Main contractor** – constructs the project with his own building team or is responsible for hiring subcontractors and specialist trades as part of the construction contract. They will schedule the works, trades and building material deliveries, and will act as the project manager.
2. **Independent project manager** – as mentioned above, this is often the main contractor. However, it could be an independent specialist who is employed by the client to administer the contract, oversee the building works and keep the project on budget and timescale – often used when a number of specialist subcontractors are needed who fall outside the remit of the main contractor. Some designers take on the responsibility of coordinating individual trades and specialist subcontractors as project manager. This requires extensive knowledge of project management, the building process and when to schedule trades. An inexperienced designer taking on this role could well prove more costly to the client and thereby any savings made by not having an experienced project manager or main contractor could easily be lost. This route also dangerously exposes the designer to issues of liability, which could prove very costly both financially and to their reputation.

Other specialist contractors and subcontractors who are often contracted separately by the client, but who need to be kept in the communication loop with the main contractor or project manager, are:

- kitchen and bathroom designers and fitters (especially catering kitchens)
- audio-visual equipment engineers
- swimming pool engineers
- landscapers and garden designers
- lighting designers and specialist installers
- safety and security installers.

A collaborative approach between the designer and contractors is by far the best way to work – learn from each other, benefit from each other's knowledge. Regular meetings, early identification and honest, open discussion of any unforeseen problems should avoid disputes later down the line.

Brinkworth have worked with the same contractors for a long time and so have developed a 'shorthand' that benefits the client in terms of both cost and time.

Rachel Bowyer, Director of New Business Development, Brinkworth[26]

Regulatory team

Depending on the scope and location of the project, several statutory consents and approvals might be needed. This section is based on the complex legislation that UK building projects need to comply with. It is likely that readers practising outside the UK will have similar regulations to work with. This section can also be used as a basis for good practice in countries where the legislation is not as stringent.

In the UK the **Construction (Design and Management) Regulations (CDM)**[27] mean that the client, designer and contractor all have duties to perform to conform to these regulations. This is quite a complex set of regulations, and the designer must fully understand them to make sure they know which projects they apply to, and how to manage the people and documentation that is required. Note that members of the British Institute of Interior design have a CDM helpline available (www.biid.org.uk), a very useful resource.

Regulatory authorities, especially Building Control, should be brought onto a project as early as possible; initially for their advice and guidance, and then to approve works if consents are needed. This will ensure that the project does not develop in a way that later proves to be against relevant regulations. Many designers who work in a particular geographic location will have developed good relations with these team members. The client will be expected to pay these people directly for any services or statutory regulatory permissions required.

In the UK the key people that *might* be involved (will vary according to size and scope of project) are:

Principal designer – this is to satisfy the CDM regulations for the UK, and is usually the lead consultant designing the project. Note that this only relates to projects that have more than one contractor involved, but can apply to domestic projects as well as commercial, institutional projects, etc. The principal designer must compile a Health and Safety file for the whole project, and includes contributions from both the client and the principal contractor, which must be kept up-to-date and passed to the client upon completion of the project.

Principal contractor – under the CDM regulations, the principal contractor must provide the designer with any relevant information that needs to be included in the Health and Safety file. They will also plan or make arrangements for preparing a construction phase plan which details how the site is run, emergency rules, protective equipment, etc.

Client – under the CDM regulations, the client must ensure that the principal designer prepares the Health and Safety file and keeps it regularly updated, and must inform the principal contractor of any relevant information that will affect how the construction site is managed. They must also ensure that the principal contractor has drawn up the construction phase plan before construction begins. They have a duty to inform the principal designer of any previous works to the building they are aware of, and if they sell or lease out the building they must pass (or copy) the Health and Safety file to the new owners. The client is responsible for the safe keeping of the Health and Safety file.

Planning officer – where planning permission is required, for example change of use of the building, extensions, new build, major external alterations. The planning officer may grant permission, or the application may be passed to a planning committee. Early discussions are important to determine whether permissions are required and what the local planning policies are.

Building Control surveyor – is either employed by the local authority or works independently as an approved inspector to ensure that the requirements of the building regulations are met. Where building regulations apply, an application needs to be made for approval, then this work is inspected and approved as building works proceed. They are generally very keen to be engaged at the early stages of the design and their knowledge and advice can be invaluable.

Conservation officer – advises on the conservation of historic buildings and building restrictions within conservation areas. They are knowledgeable about historic structures and local vernacular building methods, and are part of the planning team that approves applications for changes to listed buildings.

Fire inspector - more usually required in multi-occupancy buildings, commercial, public and institutional buildings.

Party wall surveyor – when the project shares a boundary with a neighbour who will have rights to reparation if any damage is caused to their property.

Rights of light consultant – everyone is entitled to light and if a new development or extension impinges on a neighbour's light, they are entitled to oppose the design.

Acoustic consultant – ensuring noise levels do not exceed regulated levels within specific environments, advising on how the design affects acoustics.

Documentation

A design project generates a lot of documents (digital and analogue, written and drawn) which need to be carefully filed (digital and paper). Every discussion (meetings, telephone calls and texts), decision and all correspondence (including emails), agreements and contracts must be documented with essential appropriate information, such as date, time, who was present, place of meeting, and regularly filed.

Keeping well-organised and logical project files so that documents can be found easily when needed (often at short notice) is an essential way of working for the designer, but the client can also benefit from keeping similar files so that they can keep up to date with the complexities of a design project, which in turn will help to avoid misunderstandings.

Design information, such as production drawings, schedules and specifications, should be logically filed, with revisions documented and distributed, so that the designer, client, consultants and contractors know which are the most current.

This administration of project information can be very time-consuming, so finding standard methods and templates will help keep this to a minimum. The *BIID Job Book* includes examples of most templates, schedules and documents that might be needed on a project and it saves time if many of the most used documents are set up as a templates which can be quickly completed either digitally or by hand.

The designer should keep a project notebook where notes are dated and all discussions, decisions and thoughts are recorded. These can then later be properly documented and filed (this should be done as soon as possible after the event and distributed to the people who need to know). We all think that we will remember what has been discussed at meetings, but in reality that never happens, so comprehensive notes taken during the meeting are essential. If decisions are made, or instructions are given at a meeting, when the designer gets back to the office they should immediately write to the people involved to confirm those decisions or instructions. The designer will most likely be the person who keeps track of most of the decisions, changes, instructions, etc, so it is vital that they document everything and feed agreed actions back to the relevant individuals. It is also advisable for the client to make notes during meetings and record decisions – again it all helps to avoid misunderstandings.

A good way of filing project documents[28] is either chronologically (on smaller jobs) or breaking files into sections, for example:

0. General
1. Client correspondence and formal agreement
2. Design team
3. Consents
4. Services/utilities
5. Contractor
6. Subcontractors/suppliers
7. Construction administration
8. Invoicing and payments
9. Drawings, schedules and specification files, ensuring that there is a numbering/revision system so that only the most current are used and circulated

... and more depending on the complexity of the project, for example a CDM (Construction Design and Management) file which includes the Health and Safety file if required.

Why does everything need to be documented? This is easy – to avoid disputes. If for any reason relationships start to break down, having easily accessible, legible and clearly written documentation will help to resolve the issue – hopefully quickly and without detriment to the relationship.

Design is a collaborative process, especially now when projects often require many specialists to be involved. Being successful at building good working relationships with all these people means the designer needs to know how to deal with difficult people, situations, tensions and conflict. Being able to do this, along with keeping excellent documentation, will help smooth the stressful process of a design project.

Building Information Modelling (BIM)

This is the way of the future, and it is a system that is now extensively used in the architecture and construction industries. BIM is a digital way of compiling the design, construction, specification, costing, post-occupancy and maintenance drawings and documentation in one complete package. It integrates all the individual traditional methods of documenting the design, construction and occupancy of an interior or building so that if a revision is made, for example to a plan to include a new item of furniture, that item of furniture will automatically appear, or update, in all the related documents – FF+E schedule, costing, etc. Most suppliers of materials and furniture now have downloadable BIM files that can be incorporated. To date it has been an infeasible proposal for small design companies to embrace this method of working, as the software required is expensive. However, as the technology becomes more widely used, the costs are reducing and many larger designer practices are using BIM. There are several industry-wide programmes, including Revit (Autodesk) and Vectorworks, who are industry leaders in this field.[29] This technology is improving at an amazingly fast rate, and all designers should train and develop a strategy for how to incorporate it into their practice.

Disputes

The best way to resolve disputes is to avoid them and to have a good client-designer agreement in place at the outset. Chapter 4 discusses in detail most of the issues that if not handled well might lead to a dispute – for example, payment problems or lack of strong client/designer agreement (see pp. 134 and 136). Problems should be caught early and dealt with effectively through communication: lots of listening, talking, regular updates and meetings, easy access to discussion, well-organised documentation (see above, p. 68), detailed and thorough drawings, schedules, contracts and agreements. If there is a problem, attend to it immediately, discuss it and try to resolve it directly – this is good practice for both the designer and the client.

Surprises are not good for either side, so avoid them. This means client and designer should both communicate bad news immediately and in person, discussing calmly any issues that might arise and pulling from the project's documentation if needed as evidence to try and resolve the issue without involving a third party.

Sadly, many disputes arise due to payment problems (see p. 134). Examples of this scenario could include:

- where the client disagrees with the designer's invoice for fees
- where the the client and designer cannot agree how or what to charge for additional services that the designer has provided
- if the client believes that the designer has not satisfactorily carried out the services to which they agreed.

The key to avoiding payment problems is for both the client and designer to be absolutely clear about how they will organise and handle the financial aspects of the project. The designer needs to be clear and specific about what services they are providing, how much it will cost, what their fees will be and when they will issue invoices for payment (all discussed in detail in Chapter 4). The client needs to be transparent with the designer about the budget they have available for the project, where the funds are coming from (if a third party lender is involved, the designer should be aware of this), and exactly who is responsible for clearing invoices for payment (a named person). The more open and specific both parties are, the less likely a payment dispute will arise.

There can be any number of reasons for a dispute but, as already mentioned, the first thing to do is to try and resolve it without a third party. And this is why keeping excellent records and having a thorough Scope of Design Services will help clarify issues by reminding the parties of the original agreements. Having a thorough and specific Scope of Design Services as part of the comprehensive formal client-designer agreement is also crucial if the dispute goes to adjudication, arbitration or litigation.

If the client and designer cannot resolve the issue themselves, there are several more formal routes to resolving it using methods of Alternative Dispute Resolution (ADR) which have benefits over litigation (i.e. going to court)[30] and are broadly similar in many countries. ADR is a collective term to describe three main ways of resolving disputes that do not involved litigation and courts. The overall aim of ADR is to try and maintain relationships between the disputing parties, to keep the cost of resolving the dispute to a minimum and to resolve the issue quickly. The three methods are:

1.   Mediation
2.   Adjudication
3.   Arbitration.

Mediation is where a neutral person (the mediator) helps to facilitate discussions so that the parties can mutually agree a resolution to the dispute, without the need for legal advisors, and most importantly get the relationship back on track. The aim is for both parties to be satisfied with the decision they reach – it is not a win/lose situation where a decision is imposed. The mediator does not need to be knowledgeable about the construction industry; they are expert at getting the disputing parties to communicate their side of the grievance and what would be a satisfactory outcome for them. It is usually very quick (often only a day is needed) and usually cheaper than adjudication or arbitration, and definitely much cheaper than litigation. The mediator usually talks to each party separately to understand the perception of the problem of each, and then jointly to help facilitate a resolution. The mediation process needs to be agreed to by both parties and mediators can be found through several resources (the BIID and the RIBA can recommend mediators, or a more general resource is the College of Mediators[31]).

Adjudication is specifically for construction contracts where an impartial third-party adjudicator is appointed and, after hearing evidence, will impose a resolution that is legally binding. The adjudicator is often a construction industry professional with a knowledge of law. It is a process that is designed to fast-track a solution and is a relatively quick and inexpensive way of resolving a dispute (a decision has to be made within 28 days). It is generally a win/lose route where only one party will be happy with the result, and the adjudicator has the right to award costs. It is important to bear in mind that it will be difficult to bring a relationship back on track if this route to resolving a dispute is taken. Something that designers need to be aware of is the possibility of being 'ambushed' by an unscrupulous client taking them to an adjudication. Given that a decision has to be made within 28 days (occasionally 48), this means that the designer has just days to prepare for a hearing. To avoid being totally unprepared, the designer must ensure that all documentation is kept up to date at all times during a project. The designer must not fill in time sheets or document meetings retrospectively to try and make their documentation appear comprehensive and correct – there have been several rulings where the adjudicator has ruled against designers for doing this.[32] It is prudent for both parties to take legal advice in the case of adjudication (the designer might be covered for this by their Professional Indemnity Insurance, depending on the nature of the dispute). It is for this reason that it is more expensive than mediation, and costs for expert witnesses might also need to be considered. Adjudication is not 'held in confidence', which means that the proceedings and outcomes are in the public realm and may be used in further legal claims.

Arbitration is similar to adjudication in that a person is appointed to hear the case and make a ruling. However, unlike adjudication, arbitration is held 'in confidence' which means that anything discussed during the proceedings cannot be used in further legal claims or disciplinary proceedings. Adjudication is sometimes seen as a private court, where an arbitrator hears both sides of the dispute and makes a ruling – similar to a judge in court. The ruling is legally binding, and there is usually no right of appeal to take the dispute further to litigation.

Litigation is not part of ADR, and until relatively recently was the only course of action available to resolve a dispute. ADR was introduced to reduce the drain on the court system, and to reduce the cost and time involved for the disputing parties in resolving disputes. Litigation entails highly paid lawyers, barristers and QCs being involved in a court case, with expert witnesses, court costs and investigative reports all adding to the expense. This means litigation costs can spiral out of control rapidly. This route should be avoided where possible as it will take a huge amount of both the client and designer's time, money and emotion, and the relationship will be irretrievably broken. The only people who win are the lawyers.

Business and strategy

This area of the designer's work silently underpins the creative design process. The designer needs to understand business (their own and their clients') and think strategically about their values, design philosophy (how they design) and their moral codes. It encompasses all the non-design work that needs to be taken care of to run a design project and, just as importantly, a design business. Yes, it is about accounting, business and management, and calculated thinking, but designers are entrepreneurs so need to understand business in a wider world view. As David Kester, former chief executive of the Design Council, says in his foreword to Shan Preddy's excellent book, *How to Run a Successful Design Business*,

'The more you know about business, the better you'll be at seeing the world from your clients' point of view, working out what they need and spotting opportunities for them. Do enough of that and you will win their confidence and form a really effective partnership where everyone wins.'[33]

This is not intended to be a business book: my purpose here is to demonstrate how understanding business and strategic thinking will support the creative processes and underpin both design projects and design business. It is for the reader to make themselves aware of current business trends and innovative business models, and they should be reading the financial pages as well as the creative magazines to stay abreast of current and future business and economic trends.

Alongside understanding business concepts and methods, strategic thinking about the philosophies and moral codes, the values that the designer wants to embed as the guiding principles on which to build their reputation and underpin their design work will make the business authentic and meaningful (to both the designer and their clients). This is what makes the designer special and different from the competition and will help identify the type of clients they want to work with.

Business

The designer needs to view business management as a creative pursuit. It needs to be treated like a design project so that it is constantly reviewed and can adjust to new ideas and methods. The designer should enjoy it as a creative challenge so that they design a business where they do what they want to do, want to be involved with, direct and take forward. As mentioned above, this is not a book about business, but it cannot be stressed enough that a designer considering running their own business needs this attitude to be able to withstand the challenges that will be thrust upon them.

The business world is learning from design and designers – they understand that creativity and innovation are crucial to differentiate their company and products from the competition.[34]

A study by Adobe and Forrester Consulting (2014) found that 82 percent of companies believe there is a strong connection between creativity and business results. In fact, companies that actively foster creative thinking outperform their rivals in revenue growth, market share and competitive leadership, according to the report.[35]

This is demonstrated by the growth in the design business sector and its promotion by the Creative and Cultural Skills Council (one of the Sector Skills Councils established by the UK government) to get young people working in this sector.[36]

Along with physical designers (i.e. product, graphics or interior), a new specialism of 'service design' is establishing itself where designers work with companies to improve their internal and external services and how they are delivered – there is not a tangible product or interior. Here, designers are taking their creative, inquisitive thinking into established business methods and practices and offering innovative solutions to entrenched company methods. Likewise, designers can learn a lot from business, as long as they take a creative, problem-solving, collaborative attitude to it.

Having a 'creative' attitude to business and knowledge about management is also a fundamental skill when designing for corporate clients. An understanding of how these clients manage and organise their business and people is crucial to be able to interpret their brand and design an appropriate environment for them. It means that the designer and corporate client can speak the same language and understand each other's point of view. It also provides the designer with opportunities to learn from business and apply models for managing and organising to their own business.

From freelance designer to design business

Most designers, like other entrepreneurs, follow a similar route and take the following steps in running their own businesses:

- study
- work as intern/junior designer within an established company and either progress to senior level within a company, or
- take on first independent project (perhaps in partnership with another designer)
- more projects come in, but designer is still doing majority of design work
- business grows, requiring staff (office administration and/or designers)
- designer starts to lose contact with the design part of the business
- designer is head honcho managing the business – not doing what they love
- designer takes on senior staff to manage the business (i.e. financial or operations director)
- designer goes back to creative input, developing new/repeat business, client relations.

This 'route' might take years and it will probably happen without much strategic planning until the crunch moment comes when the designer just cannot do it all, or is not very good at all aspects of running a business. This is the moment to decide whether to stay as a freelancer/sole trader, or take the plunge and take on premises, business consultants and staff, thereby upping the amount of work that is required to sustain this new business – which means having a strategy and targets for gaining new or repeat business. Everything starts to expand exponentially.

In the early start-up stages, building a trusting and honest relationship with a business consultant who is versed in working with micro-design businesses is an excellent route. They can offer the advice and guidance on strategy, management, finance and marketing that the designer probably needs but is not yet able to employ as part of the business. As the business grows and succeeds, it will probably retain specialist employees or consultants to take on these individual roles. Like so many other aspects of design, a collaborative attitude to working with an appropriate team of people will bring rewards. Once again, it is about the people and communicating, sharing knowledge and experience.

It is for these reasons that designers running their own business need to think strategically about the direction they want their business to go – they need a vision – and to clarify their design philosophy and personal moral/ethical codes – their values. These are discussed more fully below, on pp. 77–78.

However, putting vision and values aside for one second and sticking with the more practical aspects of business, Chapter 3 (see pp. 100-104) discusses how to balance time, cost and quality in relation to a design project – which is just as relevant to a design business. The principle is that most decisions to do with either a project or the designer's own business will need to consider these three things, and to try and balance them. Inevitably one will take priority but it is important to consider the impact it has on the other two.

For example:

The designer is considering revamping their online presence. They need to consider the cost of having a new website and associated social media versus the amount of time it will take to be published, and the quality of the sites (produced by consultant or in-house). So if the quality of the sites needs to be amazingly interactive with a lot of complex layers, the cost will be high, as a specialist will probably be needed and the time it takes to get it published long. Whereas, if the budget for this work is tight, the quality might be more carefully considered and simpler in approach, and the time to get published will probably be shorter.

Chapter 4: Fees and budgets (see pp. 129–135) discusses some of the more financial aspects of how to budget for projects and discusses business overheads and how these costs need to be regularly assessed and monitored in order to keep good management accounts. As I have stated previously, this is not a business book; its aim is to help the designer and client to understand basic principles that need to be considered in order to run a successful business and successful projects. There is a huge range of resources available to small businesses and some excellent books and associations that are aimed specifically at helping small design businesses.

Strategy - vision and values

A design business needs vision, otherwise it is anonymous in a sea of other design businesses. It needs to have integrity and a clear sense of purpose. Without these it will be taken on a journey without direction or destination – going whichever way the wind is blowing. It will take on any job that passes its way, regardless of what it is. This may prove a way for quick financial return, but is not a business that will last the course or bring in interesting clients and projects that give the opportunity to build a reputation for good, meaningful design. All businesses need boundaries and parameters to work within, much like a design brief which clarifies the constraints of a project and thereby opens up a creative path through the myriad of possibilities.

Clients will be attracted to a business that knows who it is, knows what it does well, and will not take on any work which devalues that. In order not to devalue their business, they need to know what their values are.

A client will not want to be associated with an aimless business; they want to be associated with the best, that all future clients will be of a similar or higher calibre. Their choice of design business will raise their status in their own world. So a clear message is required of the design business – both internally and externally – in order to connect with them. Internally meaning it has a clear set of values that underpins the methods of working and will not be compromised by the type of work taken on and how the work is handled, and externally by communicating these values by the consistent work it does.

So identifying vision is the first thing – this is the daydreaming. What is the destination for the business? This might be financial, it might be the type of clients, it might be any number of things, but it has to be the clear vision that the designer(s) (and management team, if there is one) are absolutely clear about. This is a time for fantasising, for dreaming big but specific. With a clear vision it becomes easier to define the values that need to be embedded in the culture of the business in order to achieve that vision. It is just like the beginning of a design project – it cannot go anywhere without vision.

Values are our underlying beliefs and ideologies like integrity, morals, ethics, standards and principles, attitude to the environment and people that are our world. By identifying them, the decisions about what work to take on will be easier, as it will have to be work that does not compromise these values – it will be work that the designer believes in and will contribute to achieving their vision. This inevitably means there has to be a good fit with the client's own values, otherwise there will be conflict and tension throughout the project. This relates to Chapter 3: The Benefits of Interior Design, and how important it is to have discussions with the client at the earliest to identify their values and the benefits they want to achieve for the project, the users and themselves.

Strategy is how the business uses its vision and values to create its core culture and to actually get the business going and running, and achieving the vision. This is where the marketing and financial plans come into play, where taking on the right staff who fit with the culture are identified, where they start to build relationships with clients – lasting relationships (see Chapter 4, pp. 146–158). This is where some serious strategic business advice is very useful and goes back to freelance designer to design business (see p. 75). Taking an interest in 'business' as well as design will make the difference to how a business grows and succeeds.

Design philosophy is a term often used by designers on their websites to try and describe who they are and how they work. It is another way of describing their values and how they manifest themselves on a project. It is the methodology by which the designer approaches a project and encompasses everything from the way they structure their services to the aesthetic choices they make, how they plan a space and what materials they specify. For example, if the designer's values include making the least impact on the environment as possible, or the needs of the users of the space are paramount, these values will be integrated into their design philosophy and method of working.

When many designers talk about their design philosophy, they are often mistakenly talking about their design 'style'. 'Style' is probably what most people think of when they talk about a designer's work, but this is a vague and fairly meaningless notion when considered in the context of design integrity and values. It is inevitable that the designer will have a *signature* which is recognisable in their work. However, this is very different to a style – which is more fashion-led, or because for that month they like it. A designer's signature comes from years of self-learning, understanding what is important to them and what is important to their clients – it is the manifestation of their values and attitude to life, work, the universe. There will be a continuity of signature through all their projects, but it should be able to adjust to the needs of the users and clients, and is a continuity of methodology rather than 'style'. This signature will be one of the reasons the client was attracted to them, but the client should be made aware that the designer will not reproduce a previous project for them, that each project and its criteria and constraints will create a new version of the signature. For the designer this is why they need to have clearly defined values and methodologies – this integrity is what will come through in their work and is what creates the signature. It is not about fashion and trends, it is a more sustainable way of working and thinking, and one which never loses sight of the vision.

3

The Benefits of Interior Design

Overview

This chapter examines what is meant by a 'successful project'. It does not examine the aesthetic success of a project, but focuses on the unseen, deeper and longer-lasting successes.

Interior design has long suffered from the populist view of being fashion- and trend-led, short-term, disposable and all about aspiration and making money; and, yes, there are many designers out there whose sole purpose is to make a 'fast buck' for themselves and their clients.

However, the committed *professional* designer will have a serious, meaningful and ethical foundation to their interior design work and understand that success goes deeper than what it looks like or making a profit – that their designs will benefit and enhance the lives of people and leave a positive legacy for the planet. These are the designers who make a difference, and clients would be wise to seek them out.

Success can mean many things to different people in different contexts. For most of us it probably means that we are happy with the outcome. Outcomes might be positive or negative, whereas 'benefits' is a totally positive word which makes us focus on how to prioritise what will make a project successful. Benefits are good things; things that we want to achieve.

The benefits cycle

Figure i shows how identifying and achieving benefits is an iterative process – each step informs the next step and learns from the previous one.

1. Identify with the client at the outset of the project the desired benefits that are priorities to be achieved for the project:
   - **People** – who is going to benefit?
   - **Planet** – how will the environment benefit?
   - **Profit** – what material benefits/value will be achieved?
2. Creatively interpret how these desired benefits can be designed into the scheme.
3. Focus the design and available resources (by balancing cost, quality and time) to achieve the desired benefits.

4. Assess by measuring – i.e. gathering quantifiable information, data and feedback – to see if the desired benefits have been achieved.
5. Analyse the data and feedback from Step 4 to demonstrate to clients for use on future projects and for the designer to use to improve their working practices the benefits that were achieved.

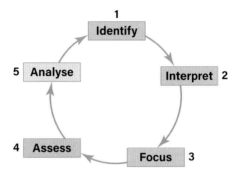

Figure i: The benefits cycle

The Three Ps[1] – benefits to people, planet and profit

The 1990s saw a subtle shift in the way businesses measured their success. Pretty much up until that point success was measured purely on financial profit, and even today this is still used as the main signifier of a successful business or project. The reason being it is the easiest to quantify and measure, and keeps a lot of accountants employed.

We are all used to hearing that the profit of a national supermarket chain is up/down by so many £millions, meaning it is in a stronger or weaker position in the financial markets, which of course satisfies its shareholders – they know whether they will be getting a dividend. However, what these measures do not account for is the impact the business is having on the planet, for example by the carbon miles the supermarket clocks up in transporting goods, or the food waste that is created because the carrots are too short or too ugly or the chemicals being put into the ground to produce the food. It also does not account for the working conditions of the people employed, either directly in their supermarkets or indirectly as suppliers from across the world.

Of course, business is much more complex than this, but generally it relies on the well-developed methods for measuring hard monetary profit to signify success which does not include the balance of the 'softer' people and planet. This is changing and, depending on the commercial sector they operate in, some businesses are developing methods for measuring benefits to the planet and people which are not data-based quantifiable methods – they are qualitative and softer, and relate to moral codes and principles rather than crunchable numbers. Interior design is a sector that should embrace the idea of the Three Ps, because what we do has such a massive impact on people and the planet.

In an ideal world, the interior designer should be able to gather data in order to demonstrate to clients why they should try to incorporate the Three Ps into their project goals and see them as a real bonus, not as something they think they should do to satisfy current ethical and 'green' thinking. However, in the real world, until some serious and ongoing research is conducted into this area of design practice that might provide standard models for measuring the benefits/success of design, it is sufficient to raise awareness of the Three Ps and try wherever possible to consider and include them in projects and initial briefing sessions with clients to help establish exactly what success means to them. Inevitably, there will always be some kind of trade-off of one for the other two, but a balance should be the aim.

My point is that whether we are a huge multi-national company, a medium-sized design business or a client buying design, we may not always be able to measure benefits, but we should always have an understanding of how what we do will benefit, rather than harm, the people involved (either directly or indirectly), the planet, and of course the bottom financial line of profit.

1. People – who is going to benefit?

It is all about people. Design is for people: for clients, for users, for makers, for manufacturers. It is people who should receive the most benefit from interior design: benefits that perhaps are not obvious and are more important, but yet more hidden, than just the aesthetic appearance. People are at the heart of everything the designer does – they are the beneficiaries. We design environments that enhance the quality of life, work and health, and the experience of the users and inhabitants.

This applies not only to those directly benefiting from the interior, but also those who have contributed to it in any way. For example, the makers, the manufacturers, the assemblers, wherever they are in the world, should all be helped, rather than harmed, in the making of the products and materials that the designer specifies.

It is the users of designed spaces that should be considered at the early stages of every project. Design can, and should, be a medium for encouraging positive change in attitudes to how we live and work. Through innovative solutions, design can encourage users to be more active, can create communities, can make life with disability easier. Designers should collaborate with both the client and users to understand their needs and how they will benefit from the scheme. It is the designer's job to explore possible benefits with the users and clients who probably do not realise or understand what might be possible.

Alongside specific benefits related to the project, there are some general benefits that good design can consistently include that should be on every designer's radar on every project, and to which clients should be alerted. These are health related – both physical and mental – and are often described by the catch-all term 'wellbeing'.

Studio TILT

NHS Whittington Hospital Trust, Ambulatory Care Centre, London, UK

Studio TILT was invited to design the unit at the Whittington Hospital following a successful collaboration between the Trust's staff, patients and management team to co-design the Outpatient Pharmacy in 2012. TILT's unique approach of co-designing spaces creates a dynamic zonal space that allows a huge range of departments to work alongside each other, from paediatrics to geriatrics, and more besides, all within a smaller footprint.

To begin the process, a programme of co-design workshops was established with representatives from all the key stakeholder groups including patients, staff and management. The workshops were facilitated by TILT and utilised its unique co-design activities and tools, helping participants to explore design ideas for the space, including layout, furniture and spatial flow. Through the process, these ideas were transformed into scaled physical prototypes by the workshop participants using basic materials such as cardboard, paper and modelling clay.

These simple prototypes were then produced professionally by TILT and used to create life-sized prototyped environments, indicative of what parts of the new ambulatory care unit would look like. These environments were then subjected to interactive testing by the hospital staff during workshops. Throughout the process, there was regular feedback of emergent data and ideas. The designs were consistently evolved as the workshop programme developed, creating a clear sense of progression for the participants. Through the whole co-design and prototyping project, over 70 people were involved, from clinicians, admin staff, the Estates Department and IT staff through to the patients themselves. Crucially, TILT's work is seen as transferable and scaleable: from workshop to prototype, from the £200,000 pharmacy project to the £3 million ambulatory care unit, all derived from a direct analysis with the end user.

The brief, concepts and the designs synthesised by TILT from the work of all the participants were very well received by everyone who took part and also by the Trust Board. TILT's methodology has demonstrated the value of engaging staff, patients and users of space in delivering public services and spaces. Project architects Levitt Bernstein delivered the space working closely with the Estates Department.

TILT's approach fitted well with the hospital's own radical approach to rethinking its estate, along with the diversification of services and service provision. As the key distinctions between hospitals and community services are being blurred, the Whittington wanted to look at ways to reposition healthcare as part of the continuum of care. Delivering these spaces with the experience and insight of those that will then deliver healthcare with them is a crucial need for the future.

Studio TILT
www.studiotilt.com

Physical health

- Accessibility for disabled users – of course there is legislation that requires designers to consider this, but it needs to go further so that inclusivity is a fundamental part of every project, not something that is purely satisfying a requirement.
- Encouraging everyone to be more active – obesity, heart disease and diabetes are steadily increasing. Design can encourage a healthier, more active attitude and could save millions in healthcare costs.

  As designers, you can help people be more active through the way you masterplan places and design the interiors of buildings. Do your designs enable or restrict physical activity? Could you design staircases that are more attractive to look at and use? Could you position them more prominently in your buildings? Are you making maximum use of 'outdoor' space, on roofs, terraces and areas immediately adjacent to your buildings, to encourage higher levels of activity and opportunities to produce or provide healthy food?[2]

- Physical needs of an ageing population – according to a UN Health Report, people aged 60 or over will outnumber children by 2047 and one in ten of us will be over 80 by 2050.[3]
- Healthy buildings – the quality of air, heat and light, non-toxic materials and sick building syndrome.

- Comfort and functional needs – fundamental basic needs, from a door handle to a workspace, have got work and they need to be comfortable.
- The working conditions of the makers and suppliers – slave workers and workers' rights to basic human needs.

Mental health

There is growing research into how people respond to, behave in and react to interiors and architecture – particularly in the retail and workplace sectors. We all know how supermarkets permeate entrance areas with the smell of freshly baked bread, how fast-food restaurants get people moving quickly through by using hard surfaces which make acoustics uncomfortable, and how product placement in retail design is based on very specific research into footfall and understanding how to manipulate customer buying habits. This is an aggressively commercial use of psychology to get customers to buy more or to increase footfall.

Studying psychology in any depth is generally not part of the designer's education. But as designers of interiors we have to look deeper than this purely commercial use of psychology and need to understand that what we build can help to improve quality of life. That how we handle circulation, manipulate spaces, colour, light and build our interiors will have an impact on the emotions of its users and how they behave. We have a very powerful role and a duty of care to consider the psychological impact of our designs on their users.

For example, some mental health and emotional issues that are becoming more important as the demographics of our world are changing:

- Happiness, satisfaction, emotional stability, boosted morale – for example, the psychology of colour and how it can impact the users of spaces and affect their feelings and behaviour. One example is the positive impact that using colour, rather than white, in prison cells has had on reducing the rates of suicide and self-harm of inmates.[4] Another is in the healthcare sector, where over 90% of nurses and all directors of nursing believe that a well-designed environment is significantly linked to patient recovery rates. They also say that the quality of hospital interiors is a significant factor when looking for a new job.[5]
- Creativity and innovation – for example, in workspaces providing sleep pods for daydreaming or encouraging staff to work away from their desks to collaborate with colleagues. Businesses recognise that innovation is what will differentiate them from their competitors, so they know they have to provide environments that promote creative and innovate thinking and habits.

▥ Universal design and inclusive living and working for all – this relates to mental health and special needs, and physical health and disability which, if well considered in all stages of design, will boost the confidence of the people affected, lessen stress and enable independence.

▥ Creating communities and encouraging connections – this might be in the workplace to encourage communication and collaboration, and in living environments to create spaces for people to meet, the inclusion of spaces where people can comfortably congregate. For example, the creation of gardens in community living developments and offices, places to grow vegetables, places to sit and chat to neighbours and colleagues.

▥ Design for the ageing population and living independently in later life.[6] We cannot avoid ageing, but designers are often in the first half of their lives and do not appreciate the needs of those in the second half of their lives. It is a truism that we do not think we will ever get old or less able. But it is inevitable, and our physical and emotional needs change as we age. Given the balance is tipping towards more people being over 60 than under in the not too distant future, attitudes to the needs of the older generations need to shift significantly.

Key beneficiaries

1. **The Client** is the most obvious beneficiary. Engaging an interior designer early in a project will produce both long- and short-term benefits for the client through innovative design solutions, by saving time and money in managing and coordinating the consultants and contractors involved, by adding value to the client's brand through gaining an understanding of their values and principles, and by understanding the needs of the users. These are just a few areas of value that an interior designer can bring to a project, and which will benefit the client by adding hard, tangible, monetary value, as well as softer, intangible integrity, meaning and feel-good factors.

However, just who is the client? A home owner, a financial director, a health committee? Their role will indicate what benefits they are looking to achieve from the design project, and it is the designer's job to question the client to find out what is motivating the project and what benefits might be achievable. It is the client that the designer needs to convince and sometimes educate into understanding there are benefits which are less obvious and measurable than just purely profit, and which extend beyond their own gain to end users.

This is why understanding benefits and value is a competitive advantage for designers. Communicating what benefits will result from the project – and especially how the client will benefit – will add winning substance and gravitas to a design proposal.

2. **The Users** are the people who will use, occupy, live, work in and experience. Here are just a few examples:

- the workforce in a workplace
- the family and children in a home
- the students in a school or college
- the patients and staff in a hospital
- the residents of a community living development
- the visitors to exhibitions
- the diners and drinkers in bars and restaurants
- the shoppers in retail stores
- the guests in hotels.

Their needs are the drivers for the project, and co-designing with them at the earliest stages of defining the brief, and putting their needs at the centre of the design, will produce successful projects. As Oliver Marlow of Studio TILT says:

'It is nothing short of arrogance to assume that we, as designers, know better than what the person who will be left using that space or sitting in that chair needs and that the stimulation from these is only in beholding them. A community is itself a creative resource, bubbling with innate skillsets, sometimes explicit but oftentimes not. The onus is therefore on the designer to establish a context and employ appropriate props or tools to engage people as co-conspirators in transforming their own environment.'[7]

This is an area of design that clients may not always appreciate – that the designer needs to observe and talk to the users to really understand their needs, rather than what the client *thinks* are their needs. To engage with the end users so that they contribute to the design process can be a time-consuming activity but it is essential to get the client onboard with this research, otherwise there is a risk that the final result will not suit the end users' needs and will be a massive waste of the client's time and money. It will reflect badly on the designer for not asking probing questions and exploring the initial brief, and could have a bad impact on their reputation.

If the users are happy, generally the client will be happy. Happy users mean a happy workforce and better productivity, happier patients who heal quicker, happier shoppers who will likely spend more money – all producing benefits for the client as well as the users.

3. **The Designer** will benefit from repeat business, increased media coverage attracting new business, increased revenues, more work that allows for the expansion of their

business – which means they can take on larger projects and perhaps work internationally – by producing interiors that fulfil (or hopefully exceed) the expectations of the client and the needs of the user. Or they may choose to stay small and offer a very personal and exclusive service.

Whichever, the benefits to the designer hinge on building reputation by the quality of the work they produce, which means satisfying all the stakeholders in the project, as well as staying true to their own values so that their work remains authentic and has integrity. Positively building their reputation is inextricably interconnected with the vision they have for their own business, their design philosophy and the ethical and moral principles that underpin their business (see Chapter 2: Business and Strategy, pp. 73–78).

4. **Trades, suppliers, contractors**, etc are a very large group of people who will benefit in a myriad of ways, depending on their role in a design project. Working with interior designers will generally mean that they are recognised for the quality of their work, and are not being engaged solely on price. Designers want to keep skills alive and should wherever possible support and patronise craftspeople and makers, and encourage their clients to do so as well. Similar to the benefits a designer achieves, the trades, suppliers and contractors benefit from doing good work that satisfies the client, designer and users. This builds reputation which builds businesses. Some of the smaller, one-man bands benefit from being connected to an interior designer who will introduce their clients to their obscure trade or skill that they otherwise would not know about.

It is not just the owners of these businesses that benefit, it is also their workers. By careful choice of supplier, designers and clients can have a direct impact on the quality of workplace conditions for these workers. By being aware of where, who and how products are being made – for example, the use of slave workers – interior design can make a difference.

2. Planet – the environment and sustainability

'The construction and operation of buildings and cities accounts for around 50% of the UK's CO_2 emissions and is thus a significant contributor to global warming. A reduction in CO_2 is needed to mitigate climate change, and this reduction is the main driver behind many building-specific EU and UK regulations, codes and frameworks. However, CO_2 emissions are not the building industry's only environmental impact. Other impacts include loss of biodiversity, resource depletion and negative effects on building users' health and well-being.'

Sophie Pelsmakers[8]

MET Studio

Climate Control, a temporary exhibition at Manchester Museum, UK, 2016

For over 30 years, experiential designers MET Studio has been planning, designing and delivering award-winning experiences for museums, expos, visitor centres, exhibitions and attractions across the world.

MET Studio's work for the Climate Control exhibition at the Manchester Museum was to avoid negative stories of climate change, focusing on giving visitors opportunities to express what matters to them whilst encouraging civic action. Climate Control, a temporary exhibition opened in May 2016, was a major contribution to Manchester's time as European City of Science 2016.

The engaging narrative for the Climate Control exhibition resulted from a close collaboration between the Manchester Museum team and MET Studio, weaving together the story of the Peppered Moth, which evolved rapidly in Manchester during the Industrial Revolution. Adapting colour to camouflage itself against the changing environment, MET Studio used the moth as a metaphor for change to link together the different exhibitions.

MET Studio was inspired by the idea of balance, cause and effect, and how small individual actions have a big collective impact. Using these as guiding principles, MET created a series of installations that suggest, 'Together we can change the future.'

Restrictions on time – six months from being commissioned to public opening – and budget led to a truly collaborative partnership. Utilising MET Studio's in-house skills, such as hand-drawn illustrations and graphic design, together with the museum's existing exhibits and artefacts ensured the limited budget was spent effectively.

MET Studio
www.metstudio.com

Interior design is a contributor to this shocking statistic and as part of the construction industry designers have to change their old habits of fashion-led, disposable, short-life interiors, and think long-term to save our planet for our children. There is no choice. We have made great progress in this area of design over the last ten years or so, but is it enough, and is it fast enough to make a difference? We cannot ignore it, we have to do more and make thinking and designing sustainably paramount to the designer's practice and to the projects they undertake. It is for the designer to educate reluctant clients to bring them on board with this attitude.

Benefiting the planet means not harming the planet, and we have to think both long- and short-term with regard to:

- environmental protection and the impact of climate change
- sustainability in reducing consumption of limited resources
- securing a future for the next generations.

The issues of the environment and sustainability have been touched on in every chapter in this book because they should be considered in every decision that is made on a design project. Designers have a big responsibility to stop using unsustainable materials or methods of manufacture that harm the environment or that result in massive waste of our precious natural resources. An attitude of re-use, recycle, retain is what will help our planet the most.

We may already be too late. Our climate is changing dramatically and much quicker than was ever anticipated. We have already seen the damage that climate change is doing to our planet – bigger and more frequent storms globally, increase of drought areas and increase of flooding are all leading to a change in food production methods, displacement of communities and loss of natural resources.

COP21 in 2015 (United Nations Conference on Climate Change)[9] resulted in a main aim to keep global warming under 2ºC. To do this requires a massive change in attitude to two key aspects of how we live and work:

1. reduce greenhouse gasses
2. embrace renewable energy sources.

How designers design and specify their interiors will have a direct impact on both of these. When choosing materials, products, furniture, fixtures and fittings we should always consider:

- The manufacturing processes involved in production – is it an energy hungry process, what type of energy is being used in the process, does it use damaging chemicals or produce toxic waste?
- The materials involved – where do they come from, are they from a sustainable source, or are they from a timber that is endangered and amongst one of the trees being felled in the Amazon rain forest? (Along with deforestation for cattle grazing and palm oil plantations, this creates other climate problems – methane produced by the cattle and the desertification of land that was once lush forests with regular rainfall.)
- The longevity of the materials, furniture, etc – quality items that can be fixed and repaired and get better with the years, rather than disposable (unless there is a very clear re-use or recycle route).
- How much travel is involved in the manufacturing and delivery process, which all adds to greenhouse gases and contamination of our seas – how many carbon miles are clocked up to get materials to manufacturer, from manufacturer to supplier, from supplier to consumer? For example, in the hypothetical making of a carpet the wool is produced in New Zealand, it gets shipped to China for cleaning, gets shipped to India for dying, gets shipped to the UK for weaving, then distributed globally to consumers. This sort of transport around the world makes no sense and we should endeavour to stop it as much as possible by not specifying this type of product and staying as local as possible.
- The amount of power products consume upon installation – heating, lighting, appliances and how careful specification can reduce this consumption.
- Reducing the need for mechanical heating and cooling systems as much as possible by utilising natural power sources and harnessing warmth and cool through appropriate insulation.

■ The manufacturers'/makers' commitment to sustainability and the environment – do they have a written policy?

These are just a few of the many issues that should be considered and will arise on most interior design projects. Designers need to be well educated in this ever-changing and fast-developing area of expertise and take an ethical stance on this area of their work so that it is an inherent and consistent attitude that underpins all projects. It is not an add-on to satisfy conscience, it is an absolute requirement for all designers to practise in this way.

So, in order for interior design to benefit the planet, it needs to:

1. Stop harming it by careful research and specification of materials, products and makers that do not harm the environment at any stage of production, and which do not use excessive amounts of energy to produce and transport.
2. Proactively consider ways of improving it by creatively re-using, recycling, retaining as much as possible, designing innovative solutions for minimising energy consumption and waste of natural resources, using local materials, products and makers – and by bringing their clients on board with this commitment.
3. At least be neutral and not contribute any more damage.

Remodelling

Interior design is usually the re-use of buildings (with the obvious exception of designing for a new build). Increasing property prices and the scarcity of land mean that existing buildings are now more valued than perhaps at any time in the past. They offer an alternative to a new build, which is costly in capital outlay. Remodelling a building is labour intensive, but it can re-use, rework and recycle the existing. Remodelling generally uses less energy and resources than a new build to construct, offering benefits to the client and the environment.

'Remodelling is the process of wholeheartedly altering a building. The function is the most obvious change, but other alterations may be made to the building itself such as the circulation route, the orientation, the relationships between spaces: additions may be built and other areas may be demolished.'
Brooker and Stone[10]

As well as the environmental benefits of remodelling buildings, their re-use has the extra benefit over a new build of an existing narrative due to the cultural and historical context that are inherent in the building and its surroundings.

Re-using will:

- benefit a building by increasing its lifespan
- be cherished by those who use and work in it
- be made safe and conform to latest standards and expectations
- contribute to the local and historic context in which it sits
- perhaps add to the regeneration of a community.

The designer needs to understand the existing building and the cultural context in which it sits and treat it with respect, yet not be a slave to the historic style and be wary of how much remodelling, intervention or design is required to make the building fit its new purpose, and to suit the client's needs.

G.A Design

Corinthia Hotel, London, UK

Opened in February 2011, The Corinthia Hotel is a grand, 294-room, five-star luxury hotel housed within the former Ministry of Defence headquarters in Whitehall, London. Seventy years of occupation by the MoD was preceded by 50 years of being the Metropole Hotel, known as a home for European royalty and London's society elite.

The brief from the client was to reinvigorate the spirit of the original Metropole while creating a new twenty-first century 'grand hotel'.

Decades of MoD use had seriously compromised the interior and as a result there was no heritage listing. The core design objective was to leave the exterior unaltered and, internally, to see beyond the chaotic MoD insertions and to recognise the original base structure.

One of the treasures of the original building was an interior courtyard. This had been filled in by the MoD, creating a very deep, dark footprint. All the infill was removed, revealing the interior façade of the original Metropole Hotel and flooding the building with new-found light.

To take advantage of this jewel at the heart of the hotel, the team designed a new, elegant central lobby lounge. Loosely taking the theme of a 'garden pavilion', the new lounge is crowned by a 9m-high glazed dome that funnels light through all the ground floor zones and from which hangs a spectacular 4m-diameter bespoke crystal chandelier, made of 1,001 crystal orbs – the figurative heart of the entire hotel.

The original ballroom from the 1800s survived relatively intact through the MoD occupation. It is now restored to its former Victorian glory while at the same time fitted with state-of-the-art technology, which required the existing ceiling to be completely removed and then reinstated by a dedicated team of plaster craftsmen, ensuring the insertions were virtually seamless.

The Northall Restaurant is a bright and airy space that occupies the 'bow' of the building. The key to this room was to maximise on the space and encourage the light through the full-height windows. Stripping out the layers of office grid ceilings from the years of MoD occupation revealed the true height and beauty of the room. During this work there was a chance discovery of a small portion of the original cornice. Only 1,000mm in length, it gave a clue to the original grand nature of the room and from this small section, the entire cornice was painstakingly re-created by plaster artisans.

Originally home to 600 guestrooms, the team took two original room footprints to create one, resulting in a new room count of 294. Original fireplaces were found throughout and, again, these were respected and have become much-loved features in many of the new guestrooms.

In keeping with the ethos of maximising the potential of the building without damage, the corner turrets of the building offered a unique opportunity to create some truly spectacular volumes. The roofing structure was carefully cut away and a new structure inserted to form double-height volumes, without any damage to the exterior of the turrets. Into those volumes the team designed seven truly individual and character-filled signature suites, the Royal Suite being the largest in Europe, and each with a spectacular private terrace overlooking London.

The hotel also features Europe's largest spa facility; at 3,300 sq m over four floors, ESPA's new flagship spa is above and below ground, using space created by excavating basement levels. Luxuriously appointed, the spa is clad in black and white veined marble and lacquered wall panels. Twelve fireplaces arranged around the entire spa complement the oyster coloured shagreen walls highlighting the richness and luxuriousness of this exclusive enclave.

G.A Design (part of the G.A Group, an integrated design solutions company) is a leading international interior and architectural design practice specialising in hospitality design worldwide.

All their projects are vastly diverse in terms of budget and style, and they are recognised worldwide for the quality of their work and ability to respond to different environments incorporating local architecture and cultural references into the concepts.

G.A Design's London studio is a community of interior architects and designers who bring creativity and talent to the drawing board. This expertise and experience in an international field, combined with the unique hotel background of the principals, enables them to produce innovative designs of the highest quality.

G.A Design
www.ga-design.com

3. Profit – adding material value

The client and everyone involved in designing and making the project will want to ensure that the project does not make a financial loss. Within the public sector there may not be a need to make a profit, but losses need to be avoided. The more commercial client will profit either in the short- or long-term through various means, for example rental return, capital value, productivity, extended life of the building or brand recognition. The designer needs to make a profit to keep their business healthy – likewise all the makers and suppliers.

Profits are the easy benefits to identify, the obvious ones. They are objective and measurable, using standard accounting and data crunching methods. Good design through innovative design solutions can have an impact on bottom-line profit for clients. Some examples are:

- increase in property capital value, rental yields and occupancy rates

- raised awareness of brand and/or reputation with resultant sales and customer loyalty
- increased retention, productivity and efficiency of workforce leading to the growth and profitability of the organisation
- healthcare recovery rates, improved learning/educational results, which results in more economical use of resources
- long-term savings in running costs by maximising the efficiency of the interior/building, and innovative use of materials and construction methods.

These are just a few examples, but it is easy to understand the main principle: interior design can add value.

However, the desire for pure financial gain to the detriment of the quality of the project and the timescale for completion will not produce *valued* projects – neither return on investment (value for money) nor valued examples of excellent design that benefit people and the planet.

The cost of a project and how much profit is made by everyone involved always needs to be considered in the contexts of quality (the quality of the build, the materials, the design) and time (lead-in times for expensive materials or products, completing on time to avoid loss of income, long- and short-term gains).

This results in a vast number of factors that will affect profit, and so perhaps a more genuine way of thinking about financial gain is to think of value – *how to achieve the best quality interior possible within the budget and timescale available, where all the stakeholders benefit* (stakeholders being the client, the users, the designer, the makers, suppliers, etc).

Achieving value means that **cost**, **quality** and **time** are intertwined – inseparable. They work in unison where one will always need to be balanced by the other two. Of course compromises will need to be made, but the aim is to be as balanced as possible.

Aiming for a balance creates a push-pull effect and this is why it is a very useful model – it makes designers and clients think about priorities. For example, if there is an incredibly tight deadline on the completion of a project, time becomes the dominant aspect that is paramount to the success of the project. This immediately sets up a series of questions of how to balance cost and quality. Will the quality of some materials need to be reconsidered because of long lead-in time? Will the quality of some materials need to be compromised and a cheaper alternative used to balance out the increased labour costs of a short timescale? Will the high cost of a material reap benefits in the long-term due to longer life expectancy or less maintenance than a cheaper material?

Figure ii: Time, cost, quality balance

These decisions need to be made without losing sight of the desired benefits for the project – to people and planet, as well as profit – whilst maintaining the integrity and ethical standards that the designer and client want to work to.

Cost

Clients are often investing large sums of money in a project and they need to feel confident that the designer will be prudent with their budget and get value for their investment. So an understanding of basic financial principles is essential for a designer because, as we have seen, cost will be a factor in nearly every decision that is made either on the project or for their business. This is discussed in more detail in Chapter 4.

Each design project will have issues which have a direct financial consequence on the cost of the project. Some major ones for both client and designer to consider are:

■ Design fees – the designer is charging for their expertise, their years of experience and knowledge, not their ability to source discounted materials, and so on.
■ Project build costs – estimating and balancing these costs with the expectations the client has for the project in terms of quality and speed of completion.

- Understanding that the complexity of construction and materials used (i.e. the language of the details) will directly impact on the cost of the project.
- Choosing and being knowledgeable about materials and the balance of quality vs durability vs longevity vs environmental standards, and how these will all impact on the final cost of the project.
- The impact on cost of a specific 'star' material – is it worth it?
- Maintenance costs upon project completion – the long-term costs.
- Cheap versus expensive and what is appropriate – materials, specialist labour, etc – for the expected lifespan of the interior.
- Operational costs for the disruption to the client's existing business and/or premises – for example, moving to temporary accommodation.
- Understanding how to present these issues to the client so they comprehend the implications to the final cost of their choices.

Quality

Quality is an overarching umbrella word that covers, for example, the sustainable qualities of a product as well as the quality of:

- a material
- workmanship
- air and light
- the space
- life.

Ideally it is paramount in the cost, quality, time triad – always strive for the best quality available in the budget and timescale.

Is quality a subjective thing? Does it come down to aesthetics or can it be more objectively assessed? Objectively, we can see when something has been poorly or well made, when the high quality of a material will outshine a lesser quality one. Subjectively, how do we assess the quality of an interior, a space? This is harder to define and is an emotive and instinctual response to how it feels – how the sunlight creates fabulous shadows, the golden proportions of the space – yet it will also include the objective qualities of how it functions and operates, how it is lit and heated.

Quality also relates to our environment, the quality of air we breathe, water we drink, our climate – and how using poor quality or inappropriate materials and method of construction will create an inferior quality of life way beyond our own immediate bubble. Improving the quality of life for those with disabilities or who are lonely or living with dementia is something we should all strive for.

Quality of design, the attention to details, to the small things that may go unnoticed by many, the things that the designer knows will improve the quality of the design that the users and clients may never consciously appreciate but which will improve the quality of their working and living environments. It is this integrity and methodology of the designer that underpins the decisions about quality to create authentic and lasting designs.

Quality is paramount to good design, so it is the designer's role to create the best possible quality designs by using quality materials, products and construction, creating lasting and authentic environments within the budget and timescale, and encouraging the client to take the same view.

Time

It is hard to move away from the cliché *time = money* because creative pursuits need time to develop and evolve. The more efficiently time is managed by everyone involved, the more cost-effective it will be for both client and designer. Designers are notorious for spending far too much time on their designs, where time evaporates and the design fee gets gobbled up, so the more efficient they are with their time management, the more likely it is that their business will be in profit.

Conversely, many clients do not appreciate how much time working up a design scheme can take, or just how long it takes to bring a project to completion. They often do not understand the complexity of a design scheme and the amount of information that needs to be communicated to get it built. So there is often a dichotomy between the client and designer, where the client expects quick results – generally due to a lack of knowledge about the design process – and the designer needs considerable time to design a scheme that incorporates the client's constraints for the project, the needs of the users and the complexities of construction imposed by the existing structure, etc. This comes down very much to the client-designer relationship and how the expectations on both sides are managed (see Chapter 4, pp. 113–115).

Repeat business can save time for everyone, as a shorthand develops in terms of communication methods, briefing and managing expectations. For example, the time the designer spends identifying the parameters of the project and understanding the client's needs in the initial stages of a project with a new client can use quite a large percentage of the design fee (often with the designer not being able to charge for all the hours worked), so it benefits both designer and client if this time is reduced. The same principle can be applied to the design and construction phases. The client should still expect to pay a premium for the designer's expertise but some savings of time can be made through repeat business.

Measuring benefits

1. **Is it necessary that we measure benefits?** There is a strong argument to support this so that designers can establish with their clients how they will measure the success of the project – the benefits that have been achieved.[11] Clients like to know what they will get out of working with an interior designer – the return they will get on their investment of money, time, emotion, energy – and it is in the designer's interest to be able to identify and illustrate these benefits.

2. **How do we measure benefits?** This is where things start to become a bit fuzzy around the edges. The interiors profession does not have an extensive history of research in gathering and analysing data to understand benefits, so it is struggling to find ways of quantifying success. We borrow from business models and architecture, but as we deal with the softer edges of the built environment and how people occupy it, to date we have not produced industry-wide methodologies. This is an area of research and professional development that probably needs to grow; however the profession has survived and thrived without it, and we will continue to successfully work instinctively with ideological and aspirational benefits that cannot be easily quantified but can perhaps be assessed in other, softer ways.

This subject was explored as one of four core tenets of a global research project in 2010/11 that the International Federation of Interior Architects and Designers (IFI) published as a document called *A Global Assessment of the Interiors Discipline*.[12] It is the result of a number of surveys, focus groups and think tanks that took place globally with designers, clients and related professionals. One section, 'Value – What are the benefits of interiors for clients, users and society?', tried to identify the value of interior design and how it can be quantified. The report concluded that at the moment there is insufficient research into this field within our profession, resulting in the lack of industry-wide methodologies and tools to enable measurement, especially of the softer values, which means it is hard to convey to clients data-based statistics that highlight the value of design. The IFI report states:

It is clear that quantification is needed in order to change and improve the public's, as well as potential clients', perceptions on the added value of design within the interior environment.[13]

The report's findings identified that essentially the benefits and value added by interiors can be divided into two categories:

1. **Quantifiable**
2. **Qualitative.**

Quantifiable examples include staff retention, workforce motivation, increased visitation and sales and brand positioning. Qualitative examples include happiness, wellbeing, pleasure and comfort. The key factor raised by the majority of contributors was the difficulty in measuring and defining 'benefits and values' (particularly the qualitative ones). It was also mentioned that

'both directly and implicitly there is a direct relationship between achieving broader qualitative goals (such as improving employee happiness or creating healthy, attractive and comfortable environments) with financial profit.'[14]

What is clear from this report is that there are no simple and obvious methods of measuring benefits. Much of what we do as designers is based on instinct and anecdotal feedback from clients and users.

Many designers do not appear to identify the client/user motivating forces at the outset of a project. They work on an intuitive basis without consciously rationalising what the desired benefits need to be in order to satisfy the client and users. More often than not this is a successful approach. However, clients are becoming more knowledgeable and demanding, and for the designer to stay strong in a very competitive market having an understanding of value and benefits might give them an advantage, and will certainly improve the likelihood of producing an appropriate scheme.

In order to measure benefits on completion of a project, desired benefits need to be identified at the start of the project. There needs to be a way of comparing ideals with actual – has the interior performed to the standard of the desired benefits?

So as Figure i (The Benefits Cycle p. 81) shows, identifying desired benefits at the start of the project is vital, as it provides a way of benchmarking and understanding the priorities for the project. Once the project is completed, it is time to get feedback, look at data and analyse it to establish whether the desired benefits have been realised. If not, why not? And how can this be improved on the next project?

The benefits that have been aimed for will direct the way in which information and data is gathered. For example, wellbeing and emotional benefits to the users will need to be examined by qualitative feedback from the users and the client (talking and observing behaviour), whereas increased footfall in a retail interior will require quantitative data gathering (numerical statistics).

It is also worth mentioning here that although this chapter focuses on project benefits, the same processes and concepts can be applied to the designer's business to assess how the team has performed, if improvements can be made to working habits to increase effectiveness, etc. If the designer is continually assessing how effective they are in operating their own business, the likelihood is that they will design, run and coordinate projects successfully.

Data and statistics

This concerns working with numbers related to the project, with input from the client and users:

- Number crunching generally and analysing data to build statistics that can put the performance of the interior into pre- and post-occupancy context. For example, increasing useable floor area by 30%, reducing energy consumption by 50%.
- Economic revenues. For example, increase in business profit, increased rental income, increased property capital value – working with the client to establish these figures.
- Client and user surveys using a numerical rating scale for answers. For example, on a scale of one to ten, do you feel less stressed in the new interior compared to the old? Or, if one is low and five is high, how does the new layout of the office contribute to collaborating with colleagues? The questions need to be very carefully phrased in order to be unambiguous.
- Post-occupancy monitoring of ongoing maintenance costs (in relation to initial outlay of material/product/installation method). For example, the long-term benefits of balancing an initial costly outlay to the reduced running costs over a period of time and the effect on the planet – i.e. aiming for carbon neutrality.

For the design business:

- Final project accounts of the cost to the design practice – has it been profitable for the practice?
- If not, analyse the numbers to see, for example, how to modify fee rates, or use of design team time on future projects.

Talking and observing

One new area of researching qualitative data in the context of interior design is social anthropology. Many large architecture and design practices are using these specialists to assist with collaborative, user-centred design by helping the designers better understand the needs of the users. As discussed on pp. 25–26 in Chapter 1, a consultant social anthropologist observes the behaviour and habits of people – both at the beginning of a project to see how they occupy spaces, move around them, conduct their jobs in them, and on completion of the project to assess if they are behaving differently, if the project has been successful in encouraging people to change ingrained ways of working to improve their effectiveness, health, happiness, etc. Social anthropologists make the art of 'people watching' into a science. They collect data on the movements and habits of people, making behaviour a measurable science. They are the professional interchange between qualitative and quantifiable research and are an incredibly useful member of the design team to work collaboratively on user-centred design.

For most projects without the resources to engage a social anthropologist, the designer needs to take on this role in a more amateur way and observe how people behave both pre- and post-project completion. For example, pre-project, to identify what benefits should be aimed for with regard to people (how they work, what equipment they need, are they able to communicate freely with colleagues, etc) and the planet (how do people abuse it and how we can change their attitudes), and post-project to see if they have been achieved.

Qualitative feedback is about talking: interviewing the client and users for their thoughts about the finished project, discussing the specific benefits that were identified as key drivers for the project, and comparing the desired benefits with those actually achieved. For example:

- Have they been achieved?
- How do the client and users know the benefits have been achieved? For example, increased productivity, less stress, greater comfort, quicker healing times (some of this is quantitative data, but getting the spoken feedback from users helps assess the intuitive responses they have to the project – how they *feel* in the interior).
- If not, can they offer ideas about how to achieve them?
- With the benefit of hindsight, are there other benefits that should have been identified?

Asking clients how the design team has performed:

- Did the client get value for money with regard to fees?
- Are there elements that could be improved in the relationship for future projects or that other clients would benefit from?
- What were the strengths and weaknesses of the methodology of the design team?
- Would they use the designer again, and why?

For the design business:

- Discuss with the design team any improvements that could be made to working practices on future projects.
- Creative discussions about what worked and what did not, identifying new ways of working and how to develop/retain client relationships.

Demonstrating benefits

Designers need to show benefits to potential clients – benefits from which the client can profit, the users will enjoy and the planet will appreciate. Documenting and analysing the quantitative and qualitative feedback from projects and using it, not just leaving it and moving on to the next project, will add integrity to the designer's practice.

Obviously this means having some great photographs of the scheme and evidence of how creative the design solution is. But what it looks like is not the only thing that will win clients. They want to know that there will be benefits from working with the designer, and the designer will want to demonstrate that the benefits go deeper than appearance and profit. The designer will probably be able to broaden the horizons of the client in terms of what benefits might be achieved, the ideals that are not dreams but can be realised through careful use of resources. This information is a key part of the designer's marketing strategy and should be incorporated into all their marketing threads – online and in print/editorial.

The methods are simple, but they need to be consistently communicated, reviewed and updated as part of the designer's practice philosophy, PR and marketing strategy:

- testimonials from clients and users
- data and statistics from similar projects that demonstrate the value interior design has added
- excellent before and after photographs

- submitting projects for awards – for recognition by the design profession, which adds a reputation to which the client will be attracted
- PR for projects – focusing on the benefits achieved, not just the glossy photos. Editorials in magazines and online forums that have an authentic message consistent with the designer's design philosophy, and demonstrate the benefits of interior design
- using social media to consistently raise recognition of the benefits of interior design
- taking potential clients to similar completed projects and meetings with other clients.

Realistic aspirational benefits alongside creative problem-solving and effective use of resources will win clients. The designer needs to prove and communicate that they can achieve this for potential clients.

The Client-Designer Relationship

4

Overview

This chapter explores how to develop, formalise and maintain good client-designer relations which are the bedrock to successful design projects, where strong collaboration and mutual respect are fundamental to producing the best possible design solution to the problem.

The key to successful relationships is to establish clear boundaries of roles, be unambiguous about what design processes will be involved, identify exactly what services the designer is providing the client and, depending on the client's level of experience working with a designer, engage in quite a lot of explaining and hand-holding to get a project built. These relationships should be viewed ideally as something that should be nurtured beyond the initial design project, for the prospect of repeat business or being introduced to potential new clients.

This chapter is divided into six sections:

1. **The client and the designer**
   - who is the client?
   - who is the designer?
   - expectations and boundaries
2. **The design process**
   - the brief, listening and egos
   - scope of the designer's work – phases, roles and services
3. **Fees and budgets**
   - what, how and when to charge
4. **Client contracts**
   - standard forms of agreement – for design services
   - other client contracts – for specialist consultants and building contractors
5. **Building relationships**
   - finding new clients
   - nurturing existing clients

The client and the designer

Who is the client?

The client could be a company, a facilities manager, a couple, someone who is not going to be the end user, or is the end user – but ultimately one or two key people must be nominated or take responsibility for commissioning the project, for appointing the designer, consultants and contractors, and to have the authority to make decisions and pay invoices.

Designers cannot expect all clients to have the same level of knowledge about how a design project proceeds from the early briefing stage to a completed interior. Some will be experienced. Others will not be and may well be apprehensive of the whole process. If the client has never commissioned a designer before, they will probably be nervous about the whole process and will need quite a bit of hand-holding, explanations and sensitivity to help them navigate this exciting, yet often stressful, process. Assume nothing. It is better to laboriously explain than to presume that the other party understands.

Depending on who the client is, the designer needs to tailor their method of working to offer an individualised service. The level of formality for the relationship needs to be assessed early on and the designer needs to gauge an appropriate level of formal versus informal communications. Whichever route is taken, even if you become the best of friends, communications must be documented and recorded, as it is still a business relationship. At some point during the project the relationship might be tested by a simple misunderstanding which, by having the relevant documentation, can be dealt with swiftly.

Clients want to feel that they are special and that the designer will provide a tailor-made solution that responds exactly to their needs. The client is the fulcrum to the project and a key member of the design team as the initiator of the project. It is they who have the insight and knowledge about their aspirations for the outcome. Their input is valuable and is what can produce great schemes. A client who is encouraged to be flexible in their thinking, who involves their end users, and who is confident to contribute and discuss ideas can help the team create unique solutions. Likewise, a good relationship also requires the client to value and trust the designer to work in their best interests.

Satisfied clients become the designer's ambassadors. Word of mouth is often the best way of securing work. As Rachel Forster, of Forster Inc, says, 'satisfied clients will come back and they spread the word.'

Who is the designer?

A company such as Brinkworth with a nominated project leader, or a smaller studio like Forster Inc, led by Rachel Forster? Whoever the designer is, the client will generally want to cultivate a personal relationship that can evolve and develop. Even if the designer is a large design company, there should be a lead designer that is the constant point of contact for the client, is present at most meetings and will deal with issues as they arise. The designer needs to make the client feel comfortable, important and valued.

Expectations and boundaries

The client will be investing often quite large sums of money into their project and will be expecting a great deal in return for that investment. Working out just what those expectations are is an essential early step to building a firm footing for what will hopefully be a long and fruitful relationship. It needs thought-provoking and investigative discussions between the client and designer to identify these expectations – the client may not have fully thought them through, but usually has an instinctive level of outcome in mind which needs to be rationalised. The designer needs to clearly identify what the client expects, and then carefully reflect on whether these expectations are realistic in terms of the design fees, budget for the build, the timescale, and the quality of build and materials (see Cost, Quality, Time balance, pp. 102–104). The designer will then need to feed back to the client whether these expectations can be met and, if not, explain what would be more realistic.

Boundaries are to set out the obligations that the client and designer each have, and for which they are mutually responsible. From the outset it is important that there is a reciprocal level of respect and trust. For example:

- The client trusts that the designer will be prudent with their budget, has the appropriate skills to satisfactorily complete the project, will be diligent in the completion of the services they have agreed to provide, will keep the client regularly informed of progress or problems, and will not make alterations to the design without the client's consent. The client also trusts that the designer is up to speed with current theories, knowledge and regulations. Most importantly, the client should be confident that the designer will be proactive throughout the project in order to fulfil, and hopefully exceed, the expectations of both the client and the end users, and make it the best that it can be.
- The designer trusts that the client will be forthcoming with all relevant information that the designer needs to be able to complete the project, will pay fees promptly upon receipt of invoices at agreed stages, has the authority to make decisions and

will do so without delay, will be available to meet at regular intervals for progress updates and approve any changes, and will appoint consultants as advised and agreed upon.

The designer should offer the client the highest standard of service and it should be personal. If working with a design company, rather than an individual designer, the client should always know exactly who they will be working with and who will be attending meetings – make it personal.

The client must understand that the designer cannot provide a guarantee that the project will be completed to the timescale and budget estimated – there are always unforeseen problems that cannot be predicted, especially when working with existing buildings, and often a contingency sum is added to the estimated cost of the build to help anticipate these costs. Costs and budgets are discussed in detail later in this chapter in the section 'Fees and budgets' (see p. 129), but perhaps it is prudent to mention here that the designer should communicate clearly and regularly with the client so that they are aware of how the budget is being spent, the impact that changes to the design will have on the final cost, and at what stages in the project they will present invoices to the client to avoid the client being billed for more than they had anticipated. The designer is also not responsible for the solvency, workmanship or products of anyone involved in the project, other than those employed or contracted directly by the designer. This applies to any other consultants that might be appointed by the client.

Essentially, the client expects that the designer can design. What they expect, and what designers need to provide, is an excellent level of service. It is not enough for a designer to presume that their creative flair and ability to get things built will be enough. Clients want to know how their money is being spent and what they can expect in return for it. In both design fees and building costs they want to know that the designer will confidently take them through what can be a demanding period of time and do an appropriate amount of hand-holding.

Fulfilling – and hopefully exceeding – the expectations of the client are what everyone involved in the project will aim for. So understanding these expectations is crucial and is why a comprehensive brief (see below, p. 116) and Schedule of Design Services (see pp. 124–128) is crucial. Unfullfilled expectations of the client can be a cause of disputes. The designer should never commit to something they cannot deliver and be explicit in what they can deliver. Ambiguity creates problems, so the designer and client should always be as honest, open and clear in their communications as possible.

The design process

The brief, listening and egos

Briefing is the start of the project, and identifies the project's motivations. Briefing sessions (of which there may be a few at various early stages of a project) are a crucial aspect of establishing a healthy and enduring client-designer relationship.

Typically, there are two briefs:

1.   **Client Brief** and
2.   **Project Brief** (also called the Design Brief)[1].

1. The **Client Brief** is the starting point, when the client says: I've got this building, this is who I am, this is what I want to do. The Project Brief is the collaborative development of the Client Brief into a working document that identifies the design approach, what the user's needs are, the drivers and motivators for the project, what benefits are desired, and how the designer will approach the project.

Presuming the client has arrived with their Client Brief, it is a fairly safe bet that this will be a simple outline of what the client wants. It is unlikely to have the detail that the designer needs to be able to work the project, so the next stage is to develop this initial information into a Project Brief. Rachel Forster describes the process with her client IDEO (see Chapter 2, pp. 58– 61):

'As a design agency IDEO had a strong idea of what they needed in their office refurbishment but they were looking for an outside person to give a different perspective. They approached me to offer a fresh pair of eyes and as an independent designer I could give unbiased advice that solved their problems without necessarily selling them products.

'When we met they had written themselves a brief. Their brief had design solutions that partly worked but didn't answer their needs completely. I went back a few steps and approached all employees with key questions to give me a sense of what was important to each individual and the team. Naturally, there were a number of factors that dictated decisions, company brand identity, spatial layout and function,employee and client experience and preference and of course budget.

'I spent time observing how they worked and moved around the office. I got an understanding of how the space had to work for them and how their clients interacted with them in the space. From this we developed a detailed Project Brief and then I presented IDEO with spatial layout ideas supported by material and furniture suggestions that represented their brand and answered their needs to create a collaborative, comfortable and creative workspace.'

2. A good **Project Brief** is the road map for the project and will help the team navigate their way through a complex series of decisions to get an interior designed and built. With a clear, detailed Project Brief, design decisions will have boundaries and will always be considered within the context of satisfying the brief. If the brief is not comprehensive and does not reflect the needs of all parties involved, it makes the design process more painful and time-consuming because too many options are possible. The brief defines constraints and limitations, narrows the options and creates a design path with signposts for decisions. Constraints are a positive thing; they should always be seen as a creative challenge by the designer that will lead them to ingenious solutions which would not have happened without the constraint.

The Project Brief needs to take into account the needs of several groups of people rather than just the client. According to Bryan Lawson, in his book *How Designers Think*,[2] there are four groups of people that generate design constraints that have varying degrees of flexibility – the most flexible being the designer, the least the legislators. The interesting point is that Lawson identifies the users as the people whose needs must be met in order for the project to be a success, with the designer and client being the people who can be flexible to meet those needs – i.e. those who can compromise:

1. Designer – flexible, optional, can shift design ideas to accommodate constraints.
2. Client – flexible, optional, can be encourage to shift ideas to meet constraints.
3. User – rigid, mandatory, must have their functional needs designed in.
4. Legislator – rigid, mandatory, designs must conform to legislation.

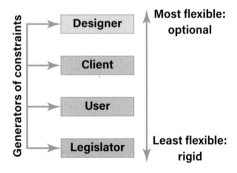

Figure iii: Generators of constraints (designed by Bryan Lawson)

Brinkworth

Residence for Dinos Chapman, Kent, UK

A pair of conjoined water reservoirs were re-appropriated by Brinkworth to create two unusual domestic residences: one for Dinos Chapman and Tiphaine de Lussy and their family, and one for a second client.

When Kevin Brennan, director of Brinkworth, discovered the reservoirs, disused and ripe for re-appropriation, he felt confident that the Chapmans would be interested in the project. Chapman describes the process of designing with Brennan as, 'Like working with my brother making art, only on paper.'

The roofed, cast-concrete boxes that comprise the reservoir are structurally made up of a concrete grid, comprising 5 sq m bays, evenly spaced with pillars. This dictates the ground floor arrangement of six rooms, with the internal walls providing support to the existing structure. Brinkworth made strategic incisions in the shell to allow daylight into the interior and cut a 30m × 5m slot into the roof to create a south-facing courtyard space. The original concrete structure has been left exposed throughout, with the exterior clad in black board-marked concrete panels, inspired by the black-timbered buildings prevalent in Kent.

Internally, warm oak flooring is used in the upper parts of the house, while polished concrete coats the ground floor space. The interior has been brought to life by de Lussy's considered, subtle styling. Her restrained choice of Scandinavian and industrial furniture pieces paired with delicately coloured fabrics add personality and individuality to the Brutalist-inspired structure.

A 74 sq m artists' studio, open-plan kitchen and living area with a 15m collapsible patio window which opens out onto the garden make up the main living and working spaces. Separating the living space from the sunken media room is a brick wall containing a double-sided, open fireplace while a central double-height atrium extension accommodates a sunken study and library. A roof terrace, lower courtyard, lap pool and rear garden provide extensive landscaped spaces.

The house has been built with sustainability and ecology in mind, and the surrounding landscape conceals a maze of sophisticated rainwater and wastewater discharge and harvesting plant, which treats the water and enables it to be circulated through the home for flushing the toilets and irrigating the garden areas. Ground source heat

pumps, concealed beneath a nearby meadow, recover natural heat from the ground and provide warm water to the under floor heating system and swimming pool. An advanced heat exchange system re-circulates the air.

Kevin Brennan says, 'Our relationship with Dinos and Tiphaine is very collaborative and we have been lucky to work with such creative and imaginative clients. It's really enabled us to push the design to the limit and create a contemporary, modernist family home.'

Brinkworth
www.brinkworth.co.uk

The views of these four key groups of people should be consulted to make the Project Brief as comprehensive and appropriate as possible. There always needs to be much discussion to dig deeper so that everyone involved understands what is driving the project, what the key motivators and priorities are, who is going to benefit and how they are going to benefit.

To be able to have these meaningful discussions the designer needs to be a good listener and should not be over-imposing their ego on the project. Inevitably, ego will be involved – designers and architects are well known for having rather large ones – but the key to a good project is the collaborative process between designer, client and users. This starts with the development of the brief which, if comprehensive, will provide the detailed information to establish the role and services that the designer will undertake and the other consultants that need to be brought on board, regulatory issues that will need to be addressed and the aesthetic design approach.

Time spent at this stage of the project and understanding the needs of all key groups is time well spent. Without a comprehensive brief, the designer might take a design path that is ultimately unfeasible, for example due to not fully understanding the needs of the client or budgetary constraints. This would impact on both the clients and designers resources due to the time required for a redesign. For example, the delay in the project might mean the client has to pay for temporary accommodation for longer than was expected, and the amount of time the designer calculated for this stage of the project when estimating his fees has been exceeded, thereby reducing their profit margin.

We enjoy constraints. Constraints on space, time and budget makes us creative.

Rachel Forster, Forster Inc[3]

Scope of the designer's work – phases, role and services

Clients might think they understand what is involved in a design project, but the designer needs to explain at length their individual process, because a novice client is unlikely to understand what processes are required of themselves, the designer, other consultants and the building contractors to get their project built. Even if the client has engaged an interior designer previously, it is very important that the designer explains step-by-step exactly what their role is, what they will be doing and when, as it may be different from how the client has engaged previous designers.

At the very outset of early discussions about the project it is better to labour the point rather than leave the client with unrealistic expectations.

Having had an initial client briefing (as discussed above) and probably a site visit, the next stage is to decide which phases of the design process will be required. The Project Brief can be developed and the designer will then be able to clearly identify their role in the project and have sufficient information to be able to pull together a comprehensive list of their services – a scope of services. This will establish exactly what the designer will do for their fee and clearly defines their input to the project so that there are no grey areas of responsibility.

It is wise to take time and be thorough in explaining the scope of services to the client, as it will demonstrate just how complex and time-consuming a project can be. Clients new to the process of design often think their project can be completed for a small cost and very quickly, while more experienced clients 'may find it reassuring to see a scope of services that clearly indicates that the designer will pay due heed to achieving cost and time targets throughout the course of the project.'[4]

Remember, ambiguity can cause disputes, so the designer needs to be clear about what they are offering, and that they are able and experienced enough to be able to complete it.

Phases

To start unravelling the scope of services the designer will undertake, the first thing to establish with the client is which phases(s) of work the designer will undertake. For example, the designer might be employed as a consultant for their design expertise and the client takes on the project from there, or the designer might be engaged to take a project from feasibility study right through to supervision of site works and handover of the completed project to the client. This is an early discussion to be had with the client and the designer needs to be clear how these parts of work are described. Different designers will probably have slightly varying ways of naming them, but essentially they are all pretty similar; it is just the boundaries of where one phase stops and another starts is a bit of a flexible feast, and how the designer feels they want to emphasise different phases of work – or break it into readily identifiable chunks – that might relate to stages for fee payments. Two examples are:

- identify problem, outline design, detail, build[5]
- discover, define, develop, deliver.[6]

Perhaps the simplest way of understanding these phases is described in the British Institute of Interior Design's Concise Agreement for Design Services CID/14,[7] which is based on the RIBA's *Plan of Work 2013*[8]. It identifies a range of services that the designer might offer, broken into just three key phases[9] of a project (discussed in detail in 'The designer's role', below):

1. **Design services** (and pre-design/feasibility)
2. **Building (including decoration) services**
3. **Furniture, Fittings and Equipment (FF+E)** services.

Designer's role

The designer might undertake all three phases or just the design and/or FF+E services. Within the design phase, the designer might only be offering feasibility, briefing, concept design, and developed design with a specialist taking on the technical design. When being appointed, the designer must make absolutely clear what role they will take during each of these three key phases of the project. By being explicit about their role, the designer will be able to clearly communicate to the client exactly what services will be undertaken and for what they are responsible, and at what point other parties take on responsibility.

1. Design services

Is the designer the lead consultant? Will they be contracted directly by the client to take responsibility for the design work, or has the designer been brought into a project to collaborate where the lead consultant is an architect? As a guide, if acting as lead consultant, the designer will be responsible, if the project requires, for:

- consulting relevant statutory authorities (planning, party wall, etc)
- coordinating the services of other consultants

- producing the design package
- reviewing progress of design work and meetings
- advising on the procurement of contractors, suppliers and FF+E
- managing changes and reporting to client.

2. **Building services**

This phase includes the designer administrating the building contract on behalf of the client with an independent third-party builder, the designer's nominated builders or the designer's in-house building team. This requires the designer to be well-versed in project management and should never be taken on by the novice designer. If undertaking building (and decoration) services, broadly speaking the designer will be responsible for:

- administering the terms of the building contract(s)
- site visits to monitor progress and quality of workmanship
- issuing payment certificates
- issuing completion certificates.

3. **Furniture, fittings and equipment (FF+E) services**

When offering these services, the designer must make one essential point very clear to the client early on – whether the designer is acting as an agent, or as a principal, which are clearly explained in CID/14:[10]

- Designer acting as agent – where the designer is acting as the client's agent and advising on the supply, procurement, delivery and/or installation of FF+E from or by others (i.e. the designer is not him/herself undertaking the supply, etc, of FF+E).
- Designer acting as principal – where the designer is him/herself supplying, procuring, delivering and/or installing FF+E.

For years the issue of how FF+E is supplied has been a grey area of what the designer does, with obscure commissions and discounts being given and received by the designer and suppliers – some of which are passed on to the client, some not. The ultimate point here is that whichever route is taken, the designer needs to know the level of liability that they are taking on if there is a defect or installation problem with FF+E that they have procured, and how they should financially account for these services. It must be totally transparent to the client.

Services

The lists of services in phases and roles, above, are not comprehensive and are only intended as an overview to the general areas of work the designer might undertake during the three main phases of a design project from feasibility to handover. We will now look in more detail at these services.

I am presuming that the designer is the lead consultant. However, even if the designer is being engaged as a consultant by, for example, an architect, this scope of services is also a good model to agree the services that the designer will provide as a consultant.

The services described by the BIID in CID/14 and the *BIID Job Book* serve as a good model at this point, as they are based on the RIBA *Plan of Work*.[11] This means that architects and interior designers are speaking the same language, and it helps to unify and professionalise the way that we describe design services to both clients and across the construction industry.

The descriptions are the core objectives that are required for each area of work. On a very large project each of the numbered stages is a clearly defined stage of work; however, on smaller projects they might be grouped/combined and this is how they are listed in the schedules of services in CID/14:

1. **Design services**
Stages 0 + 1 RIBA Plan of Work (PoW) – Pre-design/feasibility

This is before actual design work begins. These stages are where the designer gathers the information needed in order to develop the Project Brief and understand the client's motivations for the project, the benefits they want to achieve, and finding out the needs of the users, to see if it is feasible to create a good fit between what the client wants, what the users need and what the building context offers.

'0. Strategic Definition – identify the Client's brief and other core Project requirements.

'1. Preparation and brief – Develop the Project objectives including quality, sustainability aspirations, Project budget, other parameters or constraints including how FF+E is procured,and develop the Initial Project Brief, consider feasibility studies and review Site Information.'

The following list of services, which combines stages 0 and 1, is not exhaustive, and may change or expand depending on the project, but it provides a good idea of what is included at this stage:

- Visit the site/premises and carry out an initial appraisal.
- Establish the scope of works based on the client's requirements (the brief, budget and timescale).
- Carry out studies to determine the design approach (i.e. how to respond to the context and the constraints imposed by the building, budget and timescale).
- Advise on the need for services to be undertaken by other consultants or specialists.
- Advise on the client's duties under the CDM regulations.
- Advise on any necessary statutory approvals.

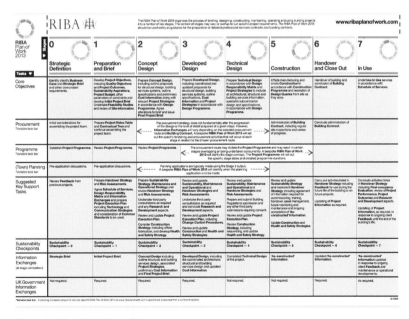

Figure iv: The RIBA Plan of Work

Stages 2, 3 + 4 RIBA PoW – Design

This is where the design work is undertaken and usually at the end of each of these three stages there will be a client sign-off to make sure that the design is fulfilling the brief – i.e. what the client wants and the users need.

'2. Concept Design – prepare concept design including outline proposals for design and specifications (and possibly preliminary cost information), along with relevant Project strategies in accordance with the Project programme. Agree on alterations to the Project Brief.

'3. Developed Design – prepare developed design including co-ordinated and updated proposals for designs and specifications, cost information and Project strategies in accordance with Project programme.

'4. Technical Design – prepare technical design in accordance with the Designer's responsibilities and in co-ordination with others instructed by the Client in relation to the Project.'

In reality these three stages often get a little muddled and merge into each other. However, it is worth bearing in mind the three distinct stages are good opportunities for a stage payment of fees and sign-off by the client before proceeding to the next stage. So what do Stages 2, 3 and 4 actually entail?

- Arrange for any necessary surveys and measured drawings to be prepared of the site/premises.
- Obtain and review existing drawings and surveys of the site/premises provided by others.
- Prepare concept design to discuss with the client.
- Prepare a developed design including, as necessary, furniture/room and electrical layouts, sample boards and visuals, and photographs or sketches of seleted furniture and fittings to discuss with the client.
- Consult with statutory authorities as necessary; advise client on any consents which might be required (i.e. applications for planning, building regulations approval, landlord's consent, party wall consent).
- Prepare a technical design for the client's approval (this might include production drawings, specifications and schedules, and coordinating designs by others).

■ Prepare an estimate of the cost of the project and a timetable for completion of the project (this should never be undertaken by the designer unless they are very experienced and knowledgeable about project management. The designer should encourage the client to engage an independent quantity surveyor or project manager for this work).

■ Prepare the client for the construction of the project (this might include reviewing with the client a suitable form of building contract for construction/installation works). Prepare building contract documentation in coordination with all members of the project team. Advise the client on a list of contractors for the project, sending out tenders and appraising tenders.

2. **Building (including decoration) services**
Stages 5, 6 + 7 RIBA PoW

'5. Construction – these services cover operations on site, including administering the terms of the building contracts where the construction is to be carried out by others than the Designer.

'6. Handover or Close out – Handover of Project and conclusion of building contract.

'7. Undertake In Use services in accordance with Schedule of Services.'

Specifically stages 5, 6 and 7 might include these services:

■ Advise the client on executing the building contract(s).
■ Administer the terms of the building contract(s).
■ At intervals appropriate to the stage of construction, visit the site/premises to monitor the progress of the design and overall quality of the building works.
■ Issue payment certificates or statements for work carried out (for the client to pay contractor).
■ Collaborate with other consultants to see that contractors/fabricators/suppliers have all information necessary for manufacture/construction/execution of all elements of the project.
■ Inspect building works at the end of any defects liability period in the building contract and arrange for any apparent defects to be remedied by the contractor.
■ Issue completion certificates in accordance with the terms of the building contract.

- Post occupancy feedback and evaluation for feeding into the benefits cycle.
- Updating project information, as requested, in response to ongoing client feedback until the end of the building's life.

Again, this list is not exhaustive, but it does give an overall idea of what services the designer might be expected to offer during the building phase of the project. The designer also needs to be very clear with the client to establish exactly what role they are taking during this phase, as discussed in 'Roles', above, on p. 122.

3. Furniture, fittings and equipment (FF+E) services

As discussed briefly in 'Roles', it is crucial for the designer to be very clear what their role is when procuring FF+E for the project – either agent or principal. I cannot recommend strongly enough that both designer and client read thoroughly pp. 7–9 of the BIID CID/14 Concise Agreement for Interior Design Services when deciding what services to offer for FF+E. The designer should also talk to their professional indemnity insurers to make sure they know the level of liability they are exposing themselves to:

'Designer acting as agent – where the designer is advising the client on supply, procurement, delivery and/or installation of FF+E – i.e. the client pays suppliers directly for FF+E and the designer's liability is minimised because the supplier is responsible for defects, delays etc not the designer.

'Designer acting as principal – where the designer is undertaking the supply, procurement, delivery and/or installation of FF+E – i.e. the client pays the designer for FF+E and the designer is liable for defects, delays, faulty goods, etc.'

Designer as agent:

- Place orders with suppliers on behalf of the client, requesting individual payments from the client to the suppliers as required.
- Place orders with suppliers on behalf of the client, making payments to the suppliers from the client's project bank account (both the client and designer should be signatories).
- Visit the site of fabrication as necessary to monitor the progress and quality of the client's FF+E.
- Monitor delivery and installation on behalf of the client.

Designer as principal:

- Provide the client with an estimate for FF+E based on a full detailed specification.
- Supply and deliver the FF+E.
- Undertake the installation of the FF+E.

Fees and budgets

During my years as an educator, the one question that without fail will be asked by all students at some point is: what do I charge, and how do I charge it? The answers are dependent on so many things that they are worthy of another book. Due to anti-competition regulations, there are no standard scales of fees, so designers have to figure this out for themselves. Working out what their expertise is worth is the tricky one, especially when starting out on their first independent projects.

Deciding what to charge, how to charge it and when to charge are not light decisions. The designer needs to spend time on this, and probably have the input of their accountant to help establish some guidelines to work within that can be used as a benchmark for different projects. What follows is going to be more useful to the novice designer and micro business, and is the most basic way of calculating fees. It is by no means a comprehensive approach as no two design practices or projects are the same and financial advice from an accountant used to working with designers should always be taken as part of the business strategy. Larger design companies will have a financial team or director who will work with the designers in pulling together a fee proposal.

What to charge

The designer's fee should not be solely estimated on the basis of what they think the client will accept, but should take into account how much they want the project and what it will cost them to produce versus what the market will tolerate. There is a perception that because designers are creatives we do this work as a passion to satisfy our own creative needs, like a fine artist, so we are happy starving in our garrets. Yes, we do this work as a passion, but designers also have businesses to run with years of education, expertise, knowledge and innovative thinking that should demand a reasonable fee – just the same as a plumber or solicitor or any other skilled professional. So the designer should never underestimate their expertise, as this is what the client is in need of.

What the designer charges should reflect what they think they are worth and take into account their experience and specialist knowledge. Likewise, it should be worked out so that they are covering the time that the whole team will spend on the project, plus business operating costs and, very importantly, building in a profit margin. To do this will require a scale of hourly charge-out rates – for the designer's own time and for those who work in-house/are employed by the designer – and which include a portion of business operating costs and a profit margin. As a most basic ratio, take the hourly rate that will actually be paid to the person and at least double it. This will probably start to cover operating costs; triple it and the designer might start to make some profit.

Obviously this is a simplistic starting point and the designer should take advice to be sure of what their charge-out hourly rates should be – the more operating costs can be kept down, the healthier the profit margins will be.

In order for the designer to know what their operating costs are, they will need a fairly exact estimate of what income is required to cover everything else to keep the business running – i.e. to pay for all the overheads that are incurred that cannot directly be charged to clients, such as rent and rates on premises, services (phones, power, heating, water, etc), business consultant fees (accountant, PR), marketing, rental or regular capital outlay to update computer equipment and software and staff salaries (including the designer's own). This is by no means a comprehensive list – an accountant will help establish these overheads – but these figures, along with a schedule of hourly rates, will be the designer's benchmark for estimating fees and is why they should always regularly review hourly rates and have up-to-date management accounts.

When a project comes in, the first thing that needs to be established is exactly what work the designer will undertake by creating a schedule of their services (as described in 'Services', pp. 124–128). They can then estimate how many man hours it will take to carry out this work (do not forget to include administrative time) and add on a contingency of say 15–20% to allow for unforeseen circumstances. Multiplying by the hourly rates for each person working on the project will provide an initial estimate of what it will cost the designer's business to do the project. (Now you can see why one reason for keeping detailed timesheets is so that you can refer to similar jobs to estimate the time needed.) This estimate is the yardstick for monitoring time spent on the project to ensure there is not an overspend in terms of time, which would reduce profit margin.

How to charge

This initial estimate of the number of man hours is the standard against which the designer can establish how to charge design fees for the project. However, before they can get to the stage of working out how many hours will be required on the project, it is essential to have a comprehensive schedule of design services, as mentioned in the previous section. However, the scope of design services cannot be thoroughly detailed without considerable time being spent beforehand with the client, being briefed and at the site to establish feasibility for the scheme. Therefore time spent on the project up to this point should probably be charged to the client on a simple hourly basis or an agreed fixed fee (worked out on how much time the designer thinks will be needed).

Once there is a full schedule of design services, and the designer and client have discussed a budget for the cost of the build (not the overall cost, which would include design and consultancy fees), it is possible to work out a fee based on a percentage of the cost of the build. The percentage charged usually varies depending on the budget and will probably decrease as the overall budget increases. Again, there are no established scales for this, but having worked out an initial estimate (as above, 'What to Charge'), the designer will be able to assess what a suitable percentage would be that will cover the project costs, operating costs and profit margin. Remember that smaller jobs can eat up proportionally more time than larger jobs, so a higher percentage is required. Also, working on this basis means that the final design fee will likely be different to the initial calculations because invariably the cost of the build will change during the course of the project (which means it could go down, as well as up).

The question of a lump sum or a fixed fee for the whole scope of design services is a potentially dangerous area for the designer and should be very carefully considered before it is agreed. The client may well feel more comfortable with this type of fee as it is a known quantity, but the nature of interior design projects generally means there are often changes as the project progresses. For example, the client may want to alter something once they start to see the reality of the design or, when working with existing buildings there are always unforseen things that arise when uncovering and exposing the existing shell and services. These variations will require more time on the designer's part which needs to be recompensed. Therefore, if these type of fees are used, there should always be a caveat in the Client-Designer Agreement (see Client contracts, p. 136) that is agreed between client and designer to ensure that changes, alterations and variations to the original proposal that the fee was based on can be charged for with agreed rates.

As mentioned, lump sum and fixed fees are often used for the initial feasibility stage of a project (Stages 0 + 1) to get to the point where a full schedule of design services can be drawn up.

Often a combination of these three main ways of charging fees (fixed fee, hourly rate and percentage) is used and will depend on the scope of the project, the budget for the build and the client's preference. For example, at feasibility stage an hourly rate or fixed fee is appropriate. Once a schedule of design services has been established, a percentage fee works well.

FF+E procurement is ideally not included in a percentage fee of the build cost. The designer needs to agree with the client whether they are acting as an agent or principal, and ensure the client understands how they will be charging for this part of the project (as set out in *BIID Agreement* above, see p. 128). The designer must be scrupulously honest with the client about discounts and handling charges – they must never try and hide this.

When to charge

The designer needs to understand basic financial principles of cashflow, profit and loss if their business is to be successful.[12]

Cashflow is the oil in a business. It is like a car, lubricating all the components so that they work smoothly, efficiently and quickly. If there is no oil the engine seizes up, irreparable damage is sustained and it will cost a lot to rectify or, worst-case scenario, will be written off – i.e. bankrupted. If money is flowing into the business at regular intervals all is good, bills get paid, staff are paid, profits are growing. If money is not flowing, everything seizes up to a point where the business is at risk. So it is vital that having established *how* the designer will charge their fees, they establish *when* they are going to charge them and explain this to the client.

The formal agreement between the client and designer should make very clear when invoices will be raised throughout the project, so that the client is clear when payments will need to be made.

It is better for both the designer and client to invoice for smaller amounts regularly throughout the duration of the project (for example, monthly), rather than issuing an invoice for a large amount at the end of the job. Smaller, regular invoices mean that the designer maintains good cashflow and can pay their expenses related to the project and business operating costs, and the client is able to manage their own cashflow better so that the funds are available for the designer's fees at the agreed payment stages. If the designer does not invoice regularly and issues an enormous invoice at the end of the project, there is the potential for an unscrupulous client to create a dispute to avoid paying the whole fee. Smaller, regular invoicing allows both the designer and the client to monitor their budgets, and if there are any disagreements, they can be dealt with swiftly when they arise, rather than at the end of the project.

The *BIID Job Book* has a very clear set of model schedules of payment and invoices, and also explains how to break down a percentage fee into smaller stage payments with adjusted payments depending on the final build cost.[13]

When working with a new client, or one from overseas, there is also an argument for a 'mobilisation fee' – i.e. a payment in advance – which will help the designer gauge how committed the client is to the project, and their attitude to paying fees. If they are not happy to do this, perhaps it is time for careful consideration of whether the project is going to be more trouble than it is worth.

For overseas clients, it might also be worth establishing a regular payment schedule that is for payment in advance of services being completed. It can be incredibly difficult to chase fees across continents.

Budgets

As part of the initial briefing conversations, the client should indicate a budget for the project. This should form part of the formal agreement, and if they are unable to do this, it should be noted in the agreement. For some reason clients can be remarkably circumspect about telling their designer a figure they have in mind for the project. Perhaps they think that if they mention it, the designer will presume that it is the minimum the client wants to spend so will work to that and probably go above it. Whereas if they do not mention a budget, they hope that the designer will estimate a figure lower than the budget they have in mind. Without an idea of the client's budget it is impossible to establish where the clients priorities lie in terms of cost, quality and time (see Chapter 3, pp. 102–104). For example, does the client want a very fast turnaround on a project, that has a short intended lifecycle, thereby perhaps requiring medium quality materials? Or is quality paramount? If after establishing these priorities and preliminary feasability work it appears that the budget is not going to be sufficient, the designer and client need to reconsider whether an adjustment in terms of the balance between cost, quality and time might solve it, or whether the client should be encouraged to increase the budget, or even that the project is unfeasible for the client's brief, priorities and chosen space. It is a delicate balance.

Whilst it is important to establish exactly how the client wants to prioritise the use of the budget, it is also vital that the client understands exactly what needs to be budgeted for and that there is a difference between the build cost and the project cost.

For example, first time clients often imagine 'the budget' to be the amount of money that is available for the construction of the project (the build cost) and do not realise the significant amount that needs to be budgeted for over and above this amount to complete the project (the project cost).

Therefore the total project budget will need to account for designer's fees, other consultants' fees, planning/regulatory applications, a contingency fee to cover all those unplanned-for things, the material costs of the build, construction/labour costs, supply and installation of FF+E, specialist bespoke items and, depending on the complexity of the project, there will be other costs that need to be included. In the UK, VAT will also have a massive impact on the budget to private clients who are not able to reclaim the VAT.

Budgets and estimating fees and costs need experienced project management input, and a novice designer should never discuss budgets for either the build or total project with a client without the support and guidance of a quantity surveyor or experienced project manager (see Chapter 2, 'The design team', pp. 63–64).

Payment problems

As discussed in 'Who is the client?' on p. 113, the designer needs to be absolutely sure they know who the person is that will be responsible for paying their invoices. For example, when the client is a company they need a named person that is responsible for signing off their invoices for payments. The designer has a responsibility to make payment as easy as possible for the client in order to keep the cash flowing. They should find out the client's normal system for paying invoices and fit in with it. For example, if the client pays invoices on the 15th of each month, then an invoice issued on the 16th will not get paid for a month and possibly cause cashflow difficulties. Invoices should be issued promptly at the agreed stages of the project, there should be no unforeseen surprises for the client, make sure there are no complaints from the client that need to be addressed first, and perhaps rather obviously, the designer should provide bank details for a transfer of funds rather than wait for a cheque in the post which has to clear.

An initial discussion between the designer and client about how the project will be funded is often a prudent step. For example, a residential client might be funding the project with a mortgage, where funds are released in stage payments. The designer and client need to establish with the lender when these fund release stages will be, so that budgets can be established for the duration of the project, and for the client to budget for the significant part of the designer's fee which will be due before the building work starts (which is usually when the lender starts to release monies) – something that needs to be addressed with the lender and client.

However, there will be times when a client either disputes an invoice or cannot pay an invoice due to a number of reasons, which could be very different for a commercial client versus a residential client. The client should endeavour at all times to ensure that they have sufficient funds to pay the designer's invoices at the agreed stages, and keep the designer informed of any potential cashflow problems which could affect the designer's business cashflow. If the client disagrees with the designer's invoice or is unclear about the services being invoiced for, they should immediately discuss this with the designer to clarify the situation and try and resolve the issue.

If a payment is not forthcoming from a client, or they dispute an invoice, what is the best way forward? In the case of non-payment, initially the designer should send a reminder – the original invoice may simply have been overlooked. If no payment arrives, the designer should call the client personally and try and find out what the problem is in a non-confrontational way – it might be a very simple reason that can be resolved quickly, or perhaps an agreement can be made for stage payments so that the designer achieves at least a drip-feed rather than nothing. Many payment problems can be resolved at this stage.

However, if at any point the client starts to say that payment is not forthcoming because they are not happy with the work completed, the designer should hear warning bells. If negligence is mentioned, the designer must immediately tell their insurers (often there are clauses in policies that state they must be informed of this within a certain number of days). At this point it is probably worth trying to discuss the problem again directly with the client – face-to-face ideally. Both parties need to stay calm and reasonable. As mentioned previously, it is better to avoid a dispute than have to resort to legal proceedings – trying to maintain a good client-designer relationship should be the aim, where both sides are relatively happy.

If this does not solve the problem, then it is time for the designer to decide how to proceed. If it is a mid-stage payment, one option is to stop work on the project until the payment is received. Otherwise, depending on the law of the country in which the designer is practising, there are several options – these are discussed in detail in Chapter 2, 'Disputes', (pp. 70–73), but there are some relevant points below that may help the designer and/or client decide which route to take.

Mediation, adjudication, arbitration or legal proceedings

All will cost money, both in terms of professional/legal fees and the time it takes to deal with the issue for both the designer and the client. This time factor will be time that is not available to the designer to work on other projects, can be very debilitating to a small design business, and it is worth bearing this in mind if either side considers taking legal proceedings. For both the client and designer, there is a potential for a triple debilitating whammy of:

- paying for legal fees for a case that might not be won
- losing potential income, and
- dealing with a lot of stress.

Mediation is a very good initial method of trying to resolve the issue. It is quick, cheaper than adjudication, arbitration or litigation, with the aim that both sides feel satisfied with the outcome. The parties in dispute find a solution to the problem with the aid of an independent facilitator, the mediator. The mediator cannot impose a resolution to the dispute; they are there to smooth discussions so that a solution that is acceptable to both parties is found. However, the solution is legally binding if a settlement agreement is signed by both parties.

Adjudication is more litigious, where either party can make a request from an accredited adjudicator to deal with their case – the adjudicator is usually a construction industry expert with an understanding of law, but is not necessarily a lawyer. Once an application has been made, the adjudicator must make a ruling within 28 days (occasionally this might be longer). The ruling is legally binding, and it is generally the case that one party wins, the other loses. Sadly, it is a fact that there are some unreasonable clients out there who have little or no intention of paying fees in full and will be looking for a reason to 'ambush' the designer with an adjudication. This is why it is essential that the designer keeps totally up-to-date and thorough documentation for the project (see Chapter 2, pp. 68–70). It will be called upon, as will the formal agreement between the client and designer.

Arbitration is often considered as a private version of going to court and is where an arbitrator is appointed and will make a ruling which is legally binding. Arbitration is 'held in confidence' so that anything discussed cannot be used in any subsequent litigation.

Litigation is where both parties retain solicitors/lawyers and apply to the court for a resolution to the problem. It will usually take an extended period of time to resolve the issue, will often be at much greater expense than either mediation or adjudication and will often result in the claimant being out of pocket, even if they win the case. It is usually much better for all concerned to consider using mediation, arbitration or adjudication before trying to sue.

Client contracts

Standard forms of agreement – for design services

A project that is undertaken without a document that records exactly what the designer is going to do, what responsibilities they are undertaking and how much they will be paid for doing it, is a project that will likely end in at least one dispute, and an unhappy client-designer relationship.

Another very strong argument for having a formal agreement is that it takes the pressure off the client-designer relationship because it establishes clear boundaries on both sides. It should eliminate possible grey areas of responsibility – of who is doing what – and will serve as a point of reference and a reminder of just what the designer has undertaken to do during the project. This is important, as projects can become quite protracted from initial briefing to completion of the designer's services, and people forget, mis-remember and create their own version of events and verbal discussion. An agreement helps to avoid these situations and disputes, and keeps the project on track.

No matter how large or small the project – a large architectural interior or a piece of furniture – there should always be a formal agreement with the client that establishes clear responsibilities, fees and expectations.

A good agreement is one that balances the expectations of the client with what the designer feels is an appropriate level of input. It is something that is beneficial to each party, as it helps to protect both so that each can be confident that they will provide and receive what is required for the project to be a success. The *BIID Job Book* explains in detail the reasons for using a formal agreement between client and designer and how to avoid risk.[14]

It may seem too formal to ask the client to enter into a contract, as they may be surprised that you are asking this of them; after all, you are 'a creative', and they often do not expect this level of business professionalism. However, it is worth considering that a client who does not want to enter into this sort of agreement may well be a client that it is better to pass by, as it might demonstrate a lack of commitment to the project and does not show a great deal of respect for what the professional interior designer does. It will also most probably lead to all sorts of problems at a later date.

It is worth noting that the designer's professional indemnity insurer may well require a formal agreement between the designer and client, and this might help to persuade a reluctant client to commit to an agreement. However, even if this is not a requirement, the formal agreement is probably one of the first things they will ask to see if a claim is made because it makes clear what liability the designer has exposed themselves to and may affect how the insurers treat a claim. Likewise, if there is a dispute and legal proceedings are taken, the terms of agreement will prove to be an essential document.

It is a fine balance to achieve an agreement that does not appear to be setting a precedent for litigation. However, we must take into account that society is now much more litigious and people are much more aware of their rights and how to take action if they feel they are not being met. So both client and designer need to bear this in mind when drawing up an agreement.

Design practices working on large and/or complex projects will probably take legal advice on contracts and agreements, but smaller practices cannot afford to do this, which is why a standard form of agreement is a very useful thing. In the UK there are two good forms:

1.   the BIID Concise Agreement for Interior Design Services (CID/14) for most commercial and residential projects, and
2.   the JCT Consultancy Agreement for a home owner/occupier.

There are pros and cons to both forms of agreement. The BIID agreement provides the opportunity to very clearly define the services that the designer will provide and serves as a good road map for the project. The JCT agreement is perhaps a little more 'friendly' for the client, due to its clear English and more discursive nature. The BIID contract does feel very 'legal' in some of its writing and there are lots of conditions that qualify the items set out in the agreement.

It should be noted that these two forms of agreement are applicable to the laws of England and Scotland. For readers working outside of this region these contracts serve as good models, but the designer and client should always seek legal advice or use a form of agreement that is applicable to the laws of the country where the project is being built, and/or where the designer's practice and client are located. For projects with cross-border relationships (for example, the site is in China, the client is located in Wales and the designer's practice is in London), legal advice from a specialist construction law solicitor on how to structure the project agreements and contracts is essential. Likewise, where the designer is unsure of any matters related to contracts and agreements it is strongly suggested that advice is taken from a specialist in construction law.

BIID Agreement CID/14

This agreement has been briefly mentioned above, but let us look at it now in more detail. The British Institute of Interior Design has a client contract, The BIID Concise Agreement for Interior Design Services CID/14, which is published by RIBA Publishing. It is described as:

'Short, clear, and easy to use, The BIID Concise Agreement for Interior Design Services (CID/14) is a simplified version of the industry standard form of interior design appointment. Now even more user friendly, this contract is suitable for all but the largest and most complex projects, ensuring a fair and balanced relationship between designer and client.'[15]

After several incarnations, the agreement that is current at the time of writing is the most easily structured and comprehensive contract for quite a wide range of interior design projects, both commercial and residential. It may not be suitable if the project is very large or complex, or if it includes a range of multi-disciplinary services outside of a fairly standard interior design project (if there is such a thing), in which case a bespoke contract might be needed. However, the structure and content of CID/14 are an excellent foundation on which to base a bespoke contract (with legal advice of course).

It is worth bearing in mind that this contract has been written as one of the RIBA's suite of publications for architecture, interior design and construction, and therefore fits with its own *Plan of Work* – which is the UK architectural model for the design/construction process. As discussed above, one of the key benefits of using this contract is the clarity for precisely stating what the scope of work is that the designer is going to do on the project, and which we have looked at previously (see p. 124).

The CID/14 pack has two booklets:

1. *The BIID Concise Agreement for Interior Design Services*, which includes:
   - Memorandum of Agreement (takes the form of a legal contract)
   - Schedule of Design Services
   - Schedule of Building (and Decoration) Services
   - Schedule of Furniture, Fittings and Equipment (FF+E) Services
   - Schedule of Fees and Expenses
   - Conditions of Agreement.
2. *Notes, Cancellation Rights and Model Letter of Appointment*, which includes:
   - Notes on the use of BIID CID/14
   - BIID CID/14 Cancellation Rights (with a model form for cancellation)
   - Letter of Appointment, in model form, which can be used as an alternative to the Memorandum of Agreement. It should be on practice stationery and takes the form of a letter which has a more personal approach than the Memorandum of Agreement.

Memorandum of Agreement or Letter of Appointment

There are two methods within CID/14 for establishing a formal contract between the client and the designer:

1. Memorandum of Agreement
2. Letter of Appointment.

Essentially, they cover the same key points, with the Memorandum being more like a contract in appearance, and the Letter being a more approachable and slightly less formal version. It is, however, equally as binding as the Memorandum.

Schedule of Services

The Schedule of Services in CID/14, which can be used with both the Memorandum and the Letter, is incredibly useful as it sets out very clearly, concisely and logically exactly what the designer is agreeing to do, and serves as a good basis for establishing fees and stages in the project when a reasonable portion of fees will be paid. The scope of services that this schedule covers is discussed in detail above (see p. 124). However, to quickly recap:

- Design Services – any one, or all, of the stages of design from initial briefing to full technical design.
- Building (including decorating) services – supervision of site works by others, or where the designer is acting as the main contractor.
- FF+E services – designer acting as agent, advising on FF+E to be supplied by others, or acting as principal by supplying FF+E.

Conditions of Agreement

A crucial element of any agreement between the client and designer, the Conditions cover all the other things that need to be agreed, i.e. obligations, photography, method of charging fees, terms of payment, expenses, intellectual property, liabilities and insurances, disputes and suspension/termination of the Agreement. They are grouped into the following headings, and it is vital that both designer and client read them carefully to understand them:

- Definitions and Interpretation – explains terminology used in the conditions
- General – mutual obligations, CDM Regulations, photography
- Designer Obligations
- Client Obligations

- Assignment and Sub-contracting (either parts or the whole of the agreement)
- Fees and Payment
- Intellectual Property and Use of Information
- Liabilities
- Insurance
- Suspension and Termination
- Dispute Resolution.

JCT Contract (Joint Contracts Tribunal) consultancy agreement for a home owner/occupier

This agreement between the client and designer is only pertinent for works to a private dwelling. However, it is an incredibly simple form of agreement, using very clear and plain English that follows a similar structure to BIID CID/14. There is also a very useful sister agreement building contract for a home owner/occupier. The two contracts work together extremely well as a straightforward, easy to understand package for the design and construction of a residential project where the client is the home owner/occupier.[16]

Other client contracts

Specialist consultants

It is the lead consultant's/designer's role to pull together the best team for the project. This might mean a structural engineer needs to be consulted, an architect or a quantity surveyor, a graphic designer, a specialist kitchen designer, an IT communications specialist/engineer or a landscape architect. Any number of these people might be required. The designer should be able to recommend people for these roles to the client, but it is the client who should formally engage them. The consultant will need their own form of client agreement to be drawn up, so that they are engaged directly and paid by the client, but usually briefed by the lead designer. They are engaged by the client so that they can offer unbiased services of their expertise, and it also means the designer takes no liability for their work.

Laurence Pidgeon

Clapham house, London, UK
Fulham house extension, London, UK

Laurence Pidgeon has been London's pre-eminent specialist kitchen designer since first establishing his Alternative Plans business. He now works more independently from his showroom in Fulham and works collaboratively with designers, architects and homeowners to create great looking and extremely functional kitchens, bathrooms and home storage. His designers are enthusiasts for both design and cooking, which gives them a foody insight and an understanding of their clients' functional needs.

Laurence says, 'The kitchen fulfils many roles in our lives. It is first and foremost a place to make meals – a food factory – it has to be efficient, safe and comfortable to work in. It is the place we spend much of our time in, where we interact with family and friends. It is the room in the house which works the hardest, sees the most traffic and use. It is the hub of the home, the centre of family life and communication.'

He uses selected ranges from the most bespoke handcrafted kitchens made with extraordinary individual craftsmanship, to products made in Europe's largest and most efficient factories at the cutting edge of new technologies and materials. He collaborates with designers and architects, where his technical and specialist design knowledge produces projects of exquisite quality, yet are deeply functional and suited to the clients' needs.

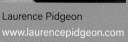

Laurence Pidgeon
www.laurencepidgeon.com

Client-contractor (the building contract)

This book is not intended as a detailed guide to project management at the construction stage of a project, or to the relationship between the client and contractor(s). However, there are a few key points that should be raised to help explain the client-contractor relationship and how and where the designer fits into it. Essentially, the designer is the intermediary between the client and contractor – however, this does not automatically mean that the designer will administrate the construction contract.

There are three key areas of decision-making where the designer can assist and advise the client on deciding the best route to get the project built:

1. **Procurement** – deciding who is going to do the building works. Simplistically there are two possible routes to take:

    (a) Where the designer is acting as the main contractor and then subcontracting to builders, electricians, plumbers, etc – this requires extensive experience of project management.

    (b) Where the client directly engages a contractor(s) – this might be a contractor that the client has used previously (difficult if the designer does not know them and the standard they build to), or when the building work has been put out to tender for three or so contractors to quote (the designer should prepare the tender documentation package and advise the client on which contractors to invite to tender, and then advise and help the client to choose the contractors based on the estimates received. Price is not the only factor in this decision – workmanship quality, timescale and structuring the building team all play a part). Sometimes the designer might have a contractor that they work with regularly and would like to nominate for the project and invite them to tender along with two others to demonstrate to the client that their estimate is fair.

Whichever route is taken, a thorough and detailed package of tender information is essential and will include drawings, schedules, specifications and sometimes a Bill of Quanities. The better the tender package in terms of information, level of detail and specification and quantities, the more accurate the estimate from the contractors. If several contractors are being asked to estimate, each contractor must be provided with exactly the same documentation in order to compare fairly the tenders received. This is why a Bill of Quantities is very useful as it helps tenderers calculate by pricing the same quantities, rather than taking quantities from drawings and specifications which might be interpreted differently. It means that all tenderers are costing exactly the same quanitites which means accurate and fair comparisons can be made to choose a contractor.

2. **Administration** – deciding who will administer the terms of the building contract (i.e. supervise works on site, sign off stages of work for payment by client, examine the standard and quality of workmanship and materials). I cannot stress strongly enough that this is not work for the novice designer. They should not undertake administering a construction contract without extensive experience of working with a project manager or someone who is experienced in administering construction contracts (i.e. a quantity surveyor or contract administrator). A novice designer does not have the knowledge to sign off stages of a build, to know that the quality of construction is appropriate, that the contractor is fulfilling his duties under his contract, or to release stage payments by the client to the contractor. It is a wiser route to encourage the client to engage a quantity surveyor (if the project is fairly large scale), a project manager or a contract administrator. However, when the designer is acting as main contractor (see BIID CID/14, p. 5), they will be responsible for the building works so they may have an in-house project manager to manage the construction (i.e. the project manager is directly engaged by the designer).

3. **Agreement** – deciding on the form of building contract between the client and the contractor(s) who will build the project. There also needs to be a separate formal agreement between the client and the person who is going to administer the building contract, for example a project manager or quantity surveyor. (If the designer is taking on this role, their work should be covered by BIID CID/14 Schedule of Building (including Decoration) Services.)

The Joint Contracts Tribunal (JCT) is the UK industry leader in standard forms of construction contract. There are several forms of contract, depending on the scope of the project and whether there is a Bill of Quantities, or any design work undertaken by the contractor, or subcontractors are required, and depends on who will administer the contract (i.e. designer, project manager, quantity surveyor). The range is pretty exhaustive and requires knowledge to understand which is the most appropriate. It is for this reason that an experienced project manager, contract administrator or quantity surveyor should be consulted when considering the procurement process and form of contract. However, as a starting point, on the JCT website there is a very useful *Guide to Selecting the Appropriate JCT Main Contract.*[17] One of their most popular contracts for smaller projects is the (JCT) Minor Works Building Contract, which is well known by the construction industry and consultants, is a standard form of contract for small projects where there is no Bill of Quantities and will very probably be appropriate to many projects undertaken by the readers of this book. There is also an accompanying document that is a very useful checklist of what needs to be considered and agreed, the *Minor Works Building Contracts (MW) 2016 User Checklist.*[18]

There is also the Home Owner Contract for small residential renovations and home building which is very clearly written to help home owners to appoint a contractor. For larger, more complex projects, then either the JCT Intermediate Building Contract or Standard Contact will probably be more appropriate and will require Bills of Quantities. Again, there are several variants depending on the types of works to be undertaken and how the contract will be administered. These are just two of the JCT family of contracts, which is broad and complex.

The 'Products' section of the JCT website provides an overview of all their contracts and much more, and is an excellent resource:[19]

The Royal Institute of British Architects also publishes its own construction contracts, which are very clear and simply laid out:

1. **The RIBA Domestic Building Contract:** 'a simple and clearly laid out contract between a customer (client) and a contractor. It is suitable for all types of non-commercial work, such as work done to the customer's own home including renovations, extensions, maintenance and new buildings.'[20]
2. **The RIBA Concise Building Contract:** 'a simple yet fully comprehensive contract between an employer (the person or organisation that wants the construction project) and a contractor. It is suitable for all types of simple commercial building work. It is not suitable for non-commercial and domestic projects.'[21]

Building relationships

The obvious ideal is for the client and designer to have a perfect working relationship that is open, honest, fulfils expectations and produces excellent finished interiors. But how does the designer find new clients, and how do clients find a designer? How do they know the relationship will be a good 'fit'? How do they cement their relationship and look to future opportunities?

For both clients and designers, it is all about the people – connecting, exploring and building relationships.

The designer – finding new clients

Designers should aim to win clients, not projects, and approach client relationships as lifelong affairs that need to be nurtured and continually reassessed – complacency will lose clients. The designer should consider themselves from their client's perspective and make sure their marketing and promotional material provides the information that a client would want to know about a designer they are considering working with.

The designer should ask for feedback from their clients, asking why they chose to work with their designer, what is successful about the relationship and what is not so good. This feedback, along with testimonials, can be constructively used to promote the designer's services to potential clients. The designer should always try and win work on their own terms – not be rushed or pressured into accepting a project without considering whether it fits with the strategic direction of their business and ethical boundaries (see Chapter 2, 'Strategy – vision and values', p. 77).

This is not a book about marketing and self-promotion. There are many others out there that will do the job better than me and, depending on the size of your business, it could be beneficial to retain a PR consultant.[22] For designers, building relationships with new clients and past clients, with journalists, with magazines and newspapers, with collaborators and with specialists is the best way to secure business. These relationships and how they develop will likely bring in more business (and the right type of business) than having an expensive marketing and PR plan alone. However, there are some essential things for you, the designer, to think about when looking for new business, to expand client lists:

1. **Do work that you believe in.** This relates to your values and the moral compass that you need to develop to know what your ethical and moral boundaries are for the clients and projects that you take on, so that you build a reputation that is authentic and sustaining (for more on this, see Chapter 2, p. 77). Aim to make the client understand what you believe in – sometimes the new 'eyes' and attitude that a designer can bring to a project helps clients perceive their project in a new way and removes some of their preconceptions and boundaries. Getting the client on board with what you believe in is a great basis for a fruitful relationship.

2. **Know why you are doing the project.** For example, is it to make money or is it to make a difference? Consider the benefits that you will get from doing the project or working with this client – make sure that all your work is constantly enhancing and strengthening your reputation. If it does not fit, do not do it.

3. **You are only as good as your work demonstrates.** Clients like looking at case studies, previous examples of your work and your credentials that make you suited to doing this project. This may include fabulous photographs of projects, but it can also mean having a clear rationale that your clients can understand, that explains how you work, the process you use and the people that might be involved.

4. **Is there chemistry?** As Rachel Bowyer of Brinkworth says, 'there has to be chemistry between us and our client.' On paper it might seem like a good fit, but have a meeting to see how your personalities fit, are they excited about your project

and how you work, do you think they would enjoy being involved and part of the team? Be sure that you know who you will actually be speaking to and who will be making decisions so that you can develop the relationship – otherwise it can all seem rather anonymous and impersonal. Trust your instinct; do not feel pressured to work with someone you do not get on with.

5. **Is it work that you are capable of doing?** This does not automatically mean that you should not take on the client/project. Sometimes it is beneficial to both client and designer to take on work that is outside their comfort zone because being naïve to the constraints of a project can bring unusual and inventive solutions. However, this means that collaboration with experts is essential in order to bring on board any specialist knowledge or skills that might be needed. Broadening the scope of your collaborations with other designers and specialists is also a way of broadening your potential for being introduced to new clients.

6. **Word of mouth.** Never underestimate it. Many of the designers I spoke to while carrying out research for this book met new clients through word of mouth – from existing clients and from collaborations with other designers and specialists. Clients often feel safer if they know someone else who has been your client, especially if they are new to working with a designer.

7. **To pitch or not to pitch for a project.** There is much discussion and debate about this. Within a more commercial context, and especially on branding projects, pitching is a common way of winning work. The Design Business Association[23] has some very good information about pitching that is invaluable. Think very carefully before you commit to a pitch – it can eat up man hours and distract from more productive projects. Essentially, there are two types of pitch: the creative pitch and the credentials pitch.

   (a) The creative pitch is where you put together some initial ideas for a specific project, usually competing with other designers who have all received the same Client Brief, and the decision is based on the design ideas presented. Some clients will expect you to do this for free – run away! Others will pay a fixed fee (which usually never covers the cost of putting the pitch together), so you have to be very sure that this is a project worth doing. Whichever, always make sure you understand who owns the intellectual property of the pitch[24] – some unscrupulous clients will take your ideas and put them into practice themselves. Creative pitches are generally not a good basis for building a client relationship because you probably do not have a chance to meet or fully understand the client or find out if you really want to work with them.

   (b) The credentials pitch, on the other hand, has a lot more going for it. This is where the designer has been given an idea of what the project is by the client, and can select case studies of their own work that address similar issues. These are then discussed with the client to demonstrate how you would approach working with them and achieving the best results for them. You can demonstrate how you work and your process by pulling out specific examples from case studies that relate to their project. It is about finding out about the people from both the client's and designer's points of view, and whether they can work together and build a lasting relationship which can develop and explore big ideas rather than one specific project. It is where you find out if there is chemistry.

8. **PR, marketing, social media.** This is where you need to make connections, meet journalists, connect with writers, magazines and online forums. The choice of which online presence to focus on is perhaps overwhelming and constantly changing, but at the very least you should have a good, clear, direct, visual website with a blog and a Twitter account. Regular posting engages a community. Videos are becoming much more important to have on your website and blog (vlog) as they engage visitors for longer, which in turn will boost your Google rating. Twitter accounts help you build relationships and see who is successfully using social media in their business. Follow journalists to find out what they are interested in and who they are talking to. This will help you to target your publicity. If you have specialist opinions or news, make sure you tell journalists about them – they are interested in people, new ideas and news, so make it easy by going to them. To be successful with PR you have to know the audiences that you want to connect to – for example, your design community (who can raise your reputation and present you with awards, which means you are easier for new clients to find) and your client's audiences (which means there is potential for new clients with similar interests or business as your existing clients). Two essential points:
    (a) make sure your facts are absolutely right, and
    (b) you always have good quality images taken of your work.
    Allocate a budget for PR and marketing. This means assigning both money and time to marketing your business and work. Up to a point you can hope that word of mouth will bring in more projects, but there will come a time when a serious and focused attitude needs to be taken. It is something that needs constant attention and – most of all – get out there, go to events and meet people!

The client – choosing a designer

This book has been written from the point of view of being a guide for both designers and clients. It works as a point of reference for clients to help them understand just what a designer does, or can do – to help get inside the head of a designer. Chapter 2, The Toolkit, will give the client a clear idea of just what services a designer can offer. Chapter 3, The Benefits of Interior Design, will help the client to understand how using a designer will add value to their project, and Chapter 4, The Client-Designer

Relationship, gives clear guidance on how to structure the designer's services and formalise the relationship. I would strongly recommend that clients read these sections during their research for a designer, and definitely before meeting them, as it will help discussions be more productive.

How do clients find a designer? This is where the designer hopes their PR, marketing and networking connects with a new client by word of mouth recommendations, reading about the designer in magazines and on social media, and most essentially having an excellent website that clients can find easily and which has relevant information for them.

Clients should research extensively potential designers when they are planning an interiors project. Talking to others who have completed a project helps enormously to understand what is involved and to get a client's point of view. By targeting projects that you like and feel would work for you, contact that client and discuss with them:

- how the project went
- how the designer performed
- any problems they had
- if it met their expectations
- what they would do differently.

If the project requires extensive structural work, look at designers who have completed this type of project, not a designer who is more of a decorator/stylist. If the project is commercial, research designers who are working in this area of design rather than solely completing residential projects.

Connecting with the national interiors association (for example, in the UK, the British Institute of Interior Design), who will generally have a section of their website which showcases their designer members. Identifying potential designers through this route will usually mean that the designer is competent and has achieved a good standard of education to be given member status. It also means that if you do engage one of their members, they must act within the association's code of conduct, which may give the client the feeling of having a safety net if there are any problems during the project.

However, it should be noted that in the UK and many other countries globally, interior design is not a regulated profession (unlike architecture), and the vast majority of designers are not members of an association such as the BIID.

The internet is a wonderful thing for researching potential designers and as a way of creating a long- or shortlist of ones being considered for the project. The next stage is to make connections with these designers to find out more about them and how they would approach the project.

For residential clients, it is likely going to be very important that there is good chemistry with the designer, where you feel the designer will guide and support you in the whole adventure – it is perhaps a more emotional decision. For commercial clients, it will be much more a hard business decision – for example, finding the designer who can best interpret their brand and create financial benefits, or who has experience designing large workplaces and is able to investigate and analyse user needs.

As a client seeking a designer it is worth reading the section above on pp. 146–149 about how designers find clients – especially the section on pitching, as this is a contenious debate in the world of design. If a pitch is considered to be the best route by the client, I cannot recommend strongly enough that it is a credentials pitch rather than a creative pitch, or somewhere in between that dangles a carrot of creativity (maybe a mood board) to open up dialogue. It is a more productive process for both client and designer, and is more likely to produce a successful scheme and relationship.

When a few designers have been shortlisted by the client, it is time to really connect with them to find out how the relationship will work. For example, if it is a large design company how is the design team constructed? Will there be one key contact designer? Do they have the skills and ability to take on the client's project? Do they have the right people in the team, or can they bring them in if needed? Do they have a proven track record in this type of project – not a must-have, but it is important that the designer can justify why they can take on this project and how they would approach it. This is not a briefing stage, it is much more a fact-finding mission of checking the designer's credentials, their past projects (going to see them, not just photographs), connecting with their other clients and finding out how they would work with the client.

Nurturing existing clients

In the long term, for both client and designer, repeat business can be incredibly useful as shortcuts can be made, the relationship is a known quantity, the amount of hand-holding that is required is understood, which can all mean cost- and time-savings. But to get to this level of trust requires consistent work on the relationship to develop it and to recognise new opportunities.

As Shan Preddy describes in her excellent book *How to Run a Successful Design Business*, the thrill of the chase for new clients is invigorating; it keeps the grey cells alive and the adrenalin rushes. But the best design solutions often come from the deeper relationships where the client and designer have a history and can work together as a team. This is the most profitable design work, as there are few steep and wasteful learning curves.[25]

So repeat business is the ideal that most designers should strive for – there is less risk as both parties know and understand how the other operates. When a project finishes, the relationship is not over – it should be viewed as ongoing. This requires serious client relationship management working alongside new business development to catch new clients. Presuming that the design business has been operating for a while and several projects have been completed, the designer will have a range of clients – current ones, potential new ones, ones that they do not want to work with again, and past ones. It is the past ones that this section is concerned with. They are the clients that offer the possibility of repeat business and are the ones with whom the designer needs to stay in regular contact.

Brinkworth

Karen Millen shops, international

Brinkworth is one of the UK's leading creative design agencies, established by Adam Brinkworth in 1990 and joined shortly after by CEO Kevin Brennan. The London-based company specialises in interior, architectural and brand design, working predominantly in retail design together with bars, restaurants, offices, residential, exhibition and events, both in the UK and internationally.

Fashion retailer Karen Millen began working with Brinkworth in 1990 to create the very first store design concepts, and the relationship has since continued to develop on a spectacular scale with more than 150 Brinkworth-designed stores worldwide. It is an extreme example of a great client-designer relationship that has evolved and developed over time, allowing a design shorthand to be used which comes from a deep understanding of the client and the brand.

The collective ambition of both client and designer to continually create premium stores is reflected by the evolution of the design showcased in two iconic retail locations, New York's 5th Avenue and London's Brompton Road in Knightsbridge. These stores, along with the others illustrated, show the diversity of design approach taken by Brinkworth over the years, with each being individually tailored to respond to their location.

Carine Roitfeld *irreverent*

This bespoke approach enables Karen Millen and Brinkworth to work much more creatively with the store environment and for each store to have a unique identity.

'Twenty-seven years on and we're still enjoying the evolution of the design of each Karen Millen store,' says Adam Brinkworth, director of Brinkworth.

Brinkworth
www.brinkworth.co.uk

Upon completion of a project the designer should make time to get some serious feedback from the client to find out their perspective of the relationship and whether the designer has fulfilled (or hopefully exceeded) their expectations. The designer needs to find out if the service they provided could be improved in any way.

Time to connect and remember past clients should be allocated by the designer as part of their new business strategy. This not only means staying in touch with the people that have been clients, it is their companies as well. News of the designer's latest projects, any new services they are offering or methods of working they are experimenting with can be interesting news to a client and can keep them engaged. The designer should stay alert to their client's current situation – both personal and company – to see if they are moving into different areas of business that might have the potential for a design project. They should also research their client's clients and contacts as well, as a way of perhaps being introduced to new clients (having an introduction is so much easier than trying to make the connection from cold). The key point is that the designer takes the initiative – keeps the relationship going, considers it long-term and does not just wait for clients to hopefully come back. Clients should always be invited to social events to stay in touch.

The majority of this book deals with how to create and build good client-designer relations, and if the concepts are used successfully, both client and designer will have a fruitful and long-term relationship.

End Notes

Defining Interiors

1   Anne Massey, *Interior Design of the 20th Century*, Thames and Hudson, London, 1994.

2   Penny Sparke and Mitchell Owens, *Elsie de Wolfe: The Birth of Modern Interior Decoration*, Acanthus Press, 2005.

3   Anne Massey, *BIID Conference 2015*, London.

4   Alvar Aalto was the first to use the natural spring of plywood in his 'Piamio' Chairs of the 1930s, Marcel Breuer designed the Long Chair in the mid-1930s, and in 1956 Charles and Ray Eames designed the Eames Lounge Chair and Ottoman for Herman Miller. In 1952 the iconic Ant Chair was designed by Arne Jacobsen, and has sold millions since it was first produced.

5   Danish designer Verner Panton was one of the most experimental designers using plastics in the 1950s and 60s. He proposed a Collapsible House (1955), a Cardboard House (1957) and a Plastic House (1960). In the early 1960s he collaborated with Vitra to design the first single-form injection-moulded plastic chair – the Panton Chair – which went into production in 1967.

6   Wally Olins, *Corporate Identity: Making Business Strategy Visible through Design*, Harvard Business School Press, Boston, 1990.

7   The advent of the low-cost airlines. Ryanair was established in 1985 and easyJet in 1996.

8   Naomi Klein, *No Logo*, Random House, Toronto , 2000.

9   *Emerging from the Global Crisis: Macroeconomic Challenges Facing Low-Income Countries*, p. 6. Prepared by the Strategy, Policy and Review Department, the Research Department, the Fiscal Affairs Department, and the Monetary and Capital Markets Department, October 2010, www.imf.org/external/np/pp/eng/2010/100510.pdf

10   www.cidq.org (accessed 25th April 2017)

11   www.rca.ac.uk/schools/school-of-architecture/interior-design/ (accessed 25th June 2016)

12   www.dezeen.com/2015/12/29/designers-as-architects-debate-opposite-of-open-minded-creativity-marcel-wanders-prefabricated-house-revolution-precrafted/ (accessed 25th April 2017)

13   The International Federation of Interior Architects/Designers (IFI) claims to be the global voice and authority for professional interior architects/designers and to represent 270,000 designers, educators and industry stakeholders in 110 countries, www.ifiworld.org

14   Ministry of Internal Affairs and Communication, Statistics Bureau, *Japan Statistical Yearbook, Chapter 2: Population and Households*, www.stat.go.jp/english/data/nenkan/1431-02.htm (accessed 25th April 2017)

15   www.pedagogyeducation.com/Long-Term-Care-Home-Health-Campus/Student-Union/Campus-News/News.aspx?news=249&cmp=H1 (accessed 25th April 2017)

16   www.archdaily.com/324418/adapt-nyc-competition-announces-micro-apartment-winner-and-finalists/ (accessed 25th April 2017)

17   www.designcouncil.org.uk/what-we-do/active-design (accessed 25th April 2017)

18   www.centerforactivedesign.org/WhatIsActiveDesign/ (accessed 25th April 2017)

19   Laura Glithero, specialist mental health care interior designer, Gilling Dod Architects, speaker at BIID Conference 2016.

20   www.youngfoundation.org/publications/benches-everyone-solitude-public-sociability-free/ (accessed 25th April 2017)

21   www.futurecommunities.net/files/images/Design_for_Social_Sustainability_0.pdf (accessed 25th April 2017

22   Interface Carpets has a mission (Mission Zero®) to eliminate any negative impact by its company on the environment by 2020, www.interface.com/EU/en-GB/about/index/Mission-Zero-en_GB (accessed 25th April 2017)

23   www.humanspaces.com/global-report (accessed 25th April 2017)

24   www.anthropology-and-architecture.net and www.gemmajohn.com

25   Dermot Egan and Oliver Marlow, *Codesigning Space*, Artifice Books on Architecture, London, 2013.

The Toolkit

1   www.contagious.co.uk/about (accessed 25th April 2017)

2   Francis D.K. Ching, *Architecture, Form, Space and Order*, Van Nostrand Reinhold Company, New York, 1979, p. 6.

3   Interview with Rachel Forster, June 2014.

4   Graeme Brooker and Sally Stone discuss re-use in detail in their book, *What is Interior Design?*

5   Graeme Brooker and Sally Stone, *Rereadings, interior architecture and the design principles of remodelling existing buildings*, RIBA Publishing, London, 2004, p. 20.

6   Drew Plunkett. *Drawing for Interior Design*, Laurence King Publishing Ltd, London, 2009, p. 6.

7   Interview with Rachel Bowyer, June 2014.

8   The British Institute of Interior Design runs a very good programme of CPD talks, as do most national interior design associations and many manufacturers and makers of products and materials.

9   This is a huge area for exploration that all ethical designers should prioritise in their work.

10   Diana and Stephen Yakeley, *The BIID Interior Design Job Book*, RIBA Publishing, London, 2010, p. 27.

11   Drew Plunkett, *Construction and Detailing for Interior Design*, Laurence King Publishing, London, 2015, p. 7.

12   HM Government, *The Building Regulations 2010 – Sanitation, hot water safety and water efficiency – Part G.*

13   HM Government, *The Building Regulations 2010 – Conservation of fuel and power – Part L.*

14   www.installation-international.com

15   Two excellent books for further research: Sofie Pelsmakers, *The Environmental Design Pocketbook*, RIBA Publishing, London, 2015; and Howard Liddell, *Eco-minimalism: the antidote to eco-bling*, RIBA Publishing, London, 2013.

16   BREEAM www.breeam.com and SEED www.seednetwork.org/about

17   Guidance on CDM Regulations 2015 are available to download from www.hse.gov.uk/pubns/books/l153.htm (accessed 25th April 2017)

18   For more information on the UK's regulations on planning consents and building regulations, see www.planningportal.gov.uk

19   See the Acknowledgements for all participants.

20   Written questionnaire set by author, completed by Jason Milne, February 2014.

21   Interview with Rachel Bowyer, June 2014.

22   Written questionnaire set by author, completed by Lori Pinkerton-Rolet, February 2014.

23   The BIID Concise Agreement for Interior Design Services (CID/14) sets out very clearly Design Services, Building Services and FF+E Services that a designer might offer.

24   The British Institute of Interior Design's Concise Agreement for Interior Design Services (CID/14) is a good template for establishing a scope of services and can be expanded upon as required.

25   The British Institute of Interior Design's Concise Agreement for Interior Design Services (CID/14) explains this in the Notes section, pp. 2–3 Building (including decoration) Services.

26   Interview with Rachel Bowyer, June 2014.

27   Available to download from www.hse.gov.uk/pubns/books/l153.htm

28   Yakeley, *The BIID Interior Design Job Book*, p. 3.

29   www.autodesk.com/solutions/bim/why-bim-and-benefits#explore (accessed 25th April 2017)

30   D. Bryan Morgan, *Dispute Avoidance, A non-confrontational approach to the management of construction contracts*, RIBA Publishing, London, 2008, pp. 11–12.

31   www.collegeofmediators.co.uk

32   Yakeley, *The BIID Interior Design Job Book*, p. 14.

33   Shan Preddy, *How to Run a Successful Design Business*, Gower Publishing Ltd, Farnham, 2011, location 244 (e-book).

34   Jon Kolko, Design 'Thinking Comes of Age', *Harvard Business Review*, September 2015, online article, www.hbr.org/2015/09/design-thinking-comes-of-age (accessed 25th April 2017)

35   Thought Leadership Paper commissioned by Adobe, *The Creative Dividend, How Creativity Impacts Business Results*, Forrester Consulting, 2014, http://landing.adobe.com/dam/downloads/whitepapers/55563.en.creative-dividends.pdf (accessed 25th April 2017)

36   www.ccskills.org.uk

The Benefits of Interior Design

1   The term 'Three Ps' was coined by John Elkington, and his 1998 book, *Cannibals with Forks: The Triple Bottom Line of 21st Century Business*, brought the concept to a wider audience.

2   The Design Council, *Active By Design*, London, 2014.

3   United Nations, *World Population Ageing 2013*, www.un.org/en/development/desa/population/publications/ageing/WorldPopulationAgeing2013.shtml (accessed 25th April 2017)

4   Discussed by Prof. Hilary Dalke at the 2014 Annual Conference of the British Institute of Interior Design.

5   Royal Institute of British Architects, *Good Design – it all adds up*, London, 2011.

6   The Design Council initiative called Independence Matters, www.designcouncil.org.uk/resources/case-study/independence-matters (accessed 25th April 2017)

7   Egan and Marlow, *Codesigning Space*.

8   Pelsmakers, *The Environmental Design Pocketbook*, p. 7.

9   www.cop21paris.org

10   Brooker and Stone, *Rereadings*, p. 11.

11   Kathryn Best, *Design Management*, AVA Publishing, Lausanne, 2006, pp. 170–73.

12   International Federation of Interior Architects/Designers (IFI), *Design Frontiers: the IFI Interiors Entity (DFIE) Phases I-III Report – A Global Assessment of the Interiors Discipline*, 2011.

13   IFI, *Design Frontiers*, p. 2.

14   IFI, *Design Frontiers*, p. 12.

The Client-Designer Relationship

1   Best, *Design Management*, p. 94.

2   Bryan Lawson, *How Designers Think*, Architectural Press, Oxford, 2000, p. 89.

3   Interview with Rachel Forster June 2014

4   Yakeley, *The BIID Interior Design Job Book*, pp. 19–20.

5   Forster Inc.

6   The Design Council.

7   British Institute of Interior Design, *The BIID Concise Agreement for Interior Design Services CID/14*, RIBA Publishing, London, 2014.

8   RIBA, *Plan of Work 2013*, www.ribaplanofwork.com

9   The responsibilities listed for these three key phases are based on *The BIID Interior Design Job Book*.

10   The British Institute of Interior Design, 'Notes on the Use of BIID CID/14', cited in *BIID Concise Agreement for Interior Design Services CID/14*, RIBA Publishing, London, 2014, p. 2.

11   The RIBA *Plan of Work* has been updated since the publication of the *BIID Interior Design Job Book* in 2010, but is still relevant to this section on services.

12   Mandy Merron, '2.6 The money (part one)', cited in *How to Run a Successful Design Business*, ed. S. Preddy.

13   Yakeley, *The BIID Interior Design Job Book*, pp. 44–45, 120, 244–280.

14   Yakeley, *The BIID Interior Design Job Book*, pp. 327–329.

15   www.biid.org.uk/about/our-publications (accessed 25th April 2017)

16   www.jctltd.co.uk/product/building-contract-and-consultancy-agreement-for-a-home-owner-occupier (accessed 25th April 2017)

17   www.jctltd.co.uk/docs/Guide-to-selecting-the-apprpriate-JCT-main-contract-Sept11.pdf (accessed 25th April 2017)

18   www.jctltd.co.uk/docs/MW-2016-User-Checklist.pdf (accessed 25th April 2017)

19   www.jctltd.co.uk (accessed 25th April 2017)

20   www.ribabookshops.com/item/riba-domestic-building-contract-2014/82643 (accessed 25th April 2017)

21   www.ribabookshops.com/item/riba-concise-building-contract-2014/82644 (accessed 25th April 2017)

22   'Section Four: The Income', in Preddy, *How to Run a Successful Design Business*, is an excellent resource.

23   www.dba.org.uk

24   A©ID – Anti Copying in Design www.acid.uk.com – is a UK-based activist organisation advising and helping designers to protect their work.

25   Preddy, '4.14 The Client Journey', *How to Run a Successful Design Business*, location 4295 (e-book).

Bibliography

Barlow, S., *Guide to BREEAM*, RIBA Publishing, London, 2011.

Beacham, C.V., McFall, B.S., Park-Gates, S., *Designing Your Future*, Pearson Education Ltd., Upper Saddle River, 2008.

Best, K., *Design Management*, AVA Publishing, Lausanne, Switzerland, 2006.

Beylerian G.M and Dent, A., *Material Connection: The Global Resource of New and Innovative Materials for Architects, Artists and Designers*, Thames and Hudson, London, 2005.

British Institute of Interior Design, *Concise Agreement for Interior Design Services*, RIBA Publishing, London, 2014.

Brooker, G. and Stone, S., *Rereadings, interior architecture and the design principles of remodelling existing buildings*. RIBA Publishing, London, 2004.

Brooker, G. and Stone, S., *What is Interior Design?*, RotoVision SA, Switzerland, 2010.

Bussey, P., *CDM 2015: A Practical Guide for Architects and Designers*, RIBA Publishing, London, 2015.

Carmichael, S., *A Guide to Successful Client Relationships*, RIBA Enterprises, London, 2002.

Ching, F.D.K., *Architecture, Form, Space and Order*, Van Nostrand Reinhold Company, New York, 1979.

Coles J. and House, N., *The Fundamentals of Interior Architecture*, AVA Publishing, Lausanne, Switzerland, 2007.

Cox, S., *A Guide to Sound Practice*, RIBA Enterprises, London, 2002.

Editor Gorb, P., *Design Management*, Architecture Design and Technology Press, London, 1990.

Elkington, J., *Cannibals with Forks: The Triple Bottom Line of 21st Business*, Capstone Publishing Ltd, Oxford, 1997 .

Evans, H., *Guide to the Building Regulations, 3rd edition*, NBS, UK, 2015.

Goslett, D., *The Professional Practice of Design*, BT Batsford Ltd., London, 1984.

Hindman, D. *Sustainable Residential Interiors, 2nd edition*, Wiley, Hoboken, 2014.

International Federation of Interior Architects/Designers (IFI), *Design Frontiers: the IFI Interiors Entity (DFIE) Phases I-III Report – A Global Assessment of the Interiors Discipline*, 2011.

Klaschka, R., *BIM in Small Practices, Illustrated Case Studies*, RIBA Enterprises, Newcastle upon Tyne, 2014.

Klein N., *No Logo*, Random House, Canada, 2000.

Kula, D. and Ternaux, E., *Materiology*, Frame Publishers, Amsterdam, 2013.

Lawson, B., *How Designers Think*, Architectural Press, Oxford, 2000.

Leydecker, S., *Designing Interior Architecture*, Birkhauser, Basel, Switzerland, 2013.

Liddell, H., *Eco-minimalism: the antidote to eco-bling, 2nd edition*, RIBA Publishing, London, 2013.

Littlefield, D., *Good Office Design*, RIBA Publishing, London, 2009.

Luder, O., *Good Practice Guide: Keeping Out of Trouble*, RIBA Publishing, London.

Massey A., *Interior Design of the 20th Century*, Thames and Hudson, London, 1994.

Morgan, D. B., *Dispute Avoidance, A non-confrontational approach to the management of construction contracts*, RIBA Publishing, London, 2008.

Olins W., *Corporate Identity: Making Business Strategy Visible through Design*, Harvard Business School Press, Boston, 1990.

Pelsmakers, S., *The Environmental Design Pocketbook*, RIBA Publishing, London, 2015.

Pile, J., *Interior Design, 3rd edition*. Pearson, New Jersey, USA, 2003.

Plunkett, D., *Construction and Detailing for Interior Design*, Laurence King Publishing Ltd, London, 2015.

Plunkett, D., *Drawing for Interior Design*, Laurence King Publishing Ltd, London, 2009.

Preddy, S. and contributors, *How to Run a Successful Design Business*, Gower Publishing Ltd, Farnham, 2011.

RIBA *Plan of Work 2013*.

Richbell, D., *Mediation of Construction Disputes*, Blackwell Publishing, Oxford, 2008.

Sparke, P. and Owens, M., *Elsie de Wolfe: The Birth of Modern Interior Decoration*, Acanthus Press, 2005.

Sully, A., *Interior Design: Theory and Process*, A&C Black, London, 2012.

The British Institute of Interior Design, *Concise Agreement for Interior Design Services (CID/14)*.

Winchip, S.M., *Sustainable Design for Interior Environments, 2nd edition*, Fairchild Books, New York, 2011.

Yakeley, D. and S., *The BIID Interior Design Job Book*, RIBA Publishing, London, 2010.

Index

Image credits

p12–15 Design, Precious McBane – all photography Thomas Stewart

p19–22 Design, Park Grove Design – all photography James Stephenson

p29 Design, MoreySmith – all photography Chris Gascoigne

p30 Design, MoreySmith – *top left* photograph Patrick Burrows,
bottom left and right photography Chris Gascoigne

p31 Design, MoreySmith – photograph Patrick Burrows

p37 Design, Brinkworth – photograph www.alexfranklin.co.uk

p45 ©Jenny Grove

p46 *all top* ©Gemma John, *all bottom* ©Forster Inc

p47 *all* © Mariane Quinn

p48 *bottom left* ©Catherine Mackey, *all other drawings* ©Jenny Grove

p59–60 Design, Forster Inc. – all photography Colin Crisford

p83–84 Design, Studio TILT – all photography Jill Tate

p85 *all top* Design Studio TILT, *all bottom* Design, Studio TILT – photography Jill Tate

p86 Design, Studio TILT – photograph Jill Tate

p91–93 Design, MET Studio – all photography Gareth Gardner –
www.garethgardner.com

p96–99 Design, GA Design – photographs reproduced by permission of the
Corinthia Hotel London

p118 Design, Brinkworth – all photography Louise Melchior

p142–143 Design, Laurence Pidgeon – all photography Darren Chung

p152–153 Design, Brinkworth – all photography Louise Melchior

p154 Design, Brinkworth – *bottom left* photograph www.alexfranklin.co.uk,
all other photographs Louise Melchior

p155 Design, Brinkworth – photograph Louise Melchior